S0-AET-614

The
GOD
of the
HOW
and
WHEN

BIBLE STUDY GUIDE I SIX SESSIONS

Kathie Lee Gifford
with Rabbi Jason Sobel

HarperChristian
Resources

The God of the How and When Bible Study Guide
© 2022 by Kathie Lee Gifford

Requests for information should be addressed to:
HarperChristian Resources, 3900 Sparks Dr. SE, Grand Rapids, Michigan 49546

ISBN 978-0-310-15654-3 (softcover)
ISBN 978-0-310-15655-0 (ebook)

All Scripture quotations are taken from the Holy Bible, New International Version®, NIV®. Copyright ©1973, 1978, 1984, 2011 by Biblica, Inc.™ Used by permission of Zondervan. All rights reserved worldwide. www.zondervan.com. The "NIV" and "New International Version" are trademarks registered in the United States Patent and Trademark Office by Biblica, Inc.™

Any internet addresses (websites, blogs, etc.) and telephone numbers in this study guide are offered as a resource. They are not intended in any way to be or imply an endorsement by HarperChristian Resources, nor does HarperChristian Resources vouch for the content of these sites and numbers for the life of this study guide.

All rights reserved. No portion of this book may be reproduced, stored in a retrieval system, or transmitted in any form or by any means—electronic, mechanical, photocopy, recording, scanning, or other—except for brief quotations in critical reviews or articles, without the prior written permission of the publisher.

HarperChristian Resources titles may be purchased in bulk for church, business, fundraising, or ministry use. For information, please e-mail ResourceSpecialist@ChurchSource.com.

First Printing November 2022 / Printed in the United States of America

Contents

A Note from Kathie Lee

Several years ago, I was in early production for a small film that I'd hoped to make here in Tennessee. I wanted a song that would capture the essence of our film. I wrote the lyrics and sent them over to my friend and songwriter Brett James to set it to music. As usual, Brett sent it right back within hours, totally ready to demo in a recording studio.

So, I called one of my favorite performers, Jimmie Allen, to record it for us, and he came right over. He nailed the song. But as it often happens, the film itself fell through, leaving us with a great song with nowhere to go. That is, unless the Lord had a different plan. And he did.

The song Brett and I had written for the ill-fated movie was already titled "The God of the How and When" and was perfectly adaptable for a brand-new oratorio by the same name.

I immediately set out to tell the stories of Abraham, Sarah, Moses, Joshua, and Mary, the mother of Jesus. They all had one thing in common: *each story represented a promise from God.* Some of those promises, however, took centuries before they were fulfilled, required a great deal of waiting from the one who had received the promise. Waiting on God is one of the hardest things for any believer. Trusting him in the process is equally as difficult. But it's in the *believing* that we truly please the God who made the promise.

In the case of Abraham and Sarah, God told Abram (his name at the time), "I will make you into a great nation, and I will bless you; I will make your name great, and you will be a blessing" (Genesis 12:2). Of course, to do this he would need an heir, which seemed impossible at the time, because his wife, Sarai (her name at the time), had been barren for many years. In fact, Sarai laughed when she heard that she would become pregnant and bear a child.

The initial promise God made to the couple took decades to come true—many decades beyond their natural child-bearing years. Their son, Isaac, was born when Abraham was one hundred years old and Sarah was ninety (see Genesis 21:1–7)!

Of course, this was the beginning of the great nation of the Hebrews that took root with Isaac's twelve grandsons. But after six hundred years of growing "as numerous as the stars in the sky" (Genesis 22:17), they were enslaved in Egypt. God made a promise to deliver them from Egypt and take them to a land of their own—the "promised" land.

But someone had to deliver them from the brutal and ruthless tyranny of Pharoah, the powerful king of Egypt. So God called an eighty-year-old shepherd from Midian who had fled Egypt decades before, instructing him to go back to the place of his birth and convince this all-powerful, evil leader to "let my people go" (Exodus 9:1). The fact that this elderly and, by his own admission, incapable man was successful in this mission is nothing short of miraculous.

The story is legendary, of course, but it continued on after Moses died and his faithful follower Joshua was called to lead the Hebrew nation to the Promised Land. Again, God's promise took decades to be fulfilled, but Joshua and the Hebrews eventually entered the land "flowing with milk and honey" (Exodus 3:8) more than forty years after leaving Egypt.

Back in the days of Abraham, God had promised the eventual father of Israel that his seed would be a blessing to all nations and that it would bring about the birth of the Eternal Deliverer, one who would be far greater than Moses (see Genesis 22:18). For centuries, the great prophets of Jehovah God prophesied this Messiah would be born of a virgin (see Isaiah 7:14). This would require a miracle even more improbable than when God parted the Red Sea.

Nevertheless, "when the set time had fully come, God sent his Son, born of a woman . . . that we might receive adoption to sonship" (Galatians 4:4). An angel visited a young woman named Mary and told her that she would be that virgin who would give birth to the promised Messiah. Nine months later, the Savior of the world came into the physical world that he had already created with his Father in the beginning.

The God of the how and when is still building his Kingdom through the lives of the billions of followers of Jesus (Yeshua), the Savior of all of humankind.

Blessed be his holy name.

How to Use This Guide

The Lord once told an ancient Hebrew prophet, "My thoughts are not your thoughts, neither are your ways my ways . . . as the heavens are higher than the earth, so are my ways higher than your ways and my thoughts than your thoughts" (Isaiah 55:8–9). The Bible is clear that God executes his own plans in his own timing. But this often trips us up, because we not only want to know *how* he is working on our behalf but also *when* he will deliver on our requests.

In this study, we will draw on the stories of five people in Scripture—Abraham, Sarah, Moses, Joshua, and Mary, the mother of Jesus—who also must have wondered *how* and *when* God would come through and deliver on his promises to them. Each of these individuals had to step out in *faith* and *obey* God without knowing all the details of what would eventually happen in their story. As we study their examples, we will discover what it really means to trust that God's ways are higher than our ways—and what it takes to truly trust in him.

Before you begin, keep in mind there are a few ways you can go through this material. You can experience this study with others in a group (such as a Bible study, Sunday school class, or any other small-group gathering), or you may choose to go through the content on your own. Either way, know that the videos for each session are available for you to view at any time by following the instructions provided on the inside cover of this study guide.

Group Study

Each of the sessions are divided into two parts: (1) a group study section, and (2) a personal study section. The group study section is intended to provide a basic framework on how to open your time together, get the most out of the video content, and discuss the key ideas together that were presented in the teaching. Each session includes the following:

- **Welcome:** A short note about the topic of the session for you to read on your own before you meet together as a group.
- **Connect:** A few icebreaker questions to get you and your group members thinking about the topic and interacting with each other.

- **Watch:** An outline of the key points that will be covered in each video teaching to help you follow along, stay engaged, and take notes.
- **Discuss:** Questions to help your group reflect on the material presented and apply it to your lives. In each session, you will be given four "suggested" questions and four "additional" questions to use as time allows.
- **Respond:** A short personal exercise to help reinforce the key ideas.
- **Pray:** A place for you to record prayer requests and praises for the week.

If you are doing this study in a group, make sure you have your own copy of this study guide so you can write down your thoughts, responses, and reflections and have access to the videos via streaming. You will also want to have a copy of the *God of the Way* book, as reading it alongside the curriculum will provide you with deeper insights. (See the notes at the beginning of each group session and personal study section on which chapters of the book you should read before the next group session.) Finally, keep these points in mind:

- **Facilitation:** If you are doing this study in a group, you will want to appoint someone to serve as a facilitator. This person will be responsible for starting the video and keeping track of time during discussions and activities. If *you* have been chosen for this role, there are some resources in the back of this guide that can help you lead your group through the study.

- **Faithfulness:** Your small group is a place where tremendous growth can happen as you reflect on the Bible, ask questions, and learn what God is doing in other people's lives. For this reason, be fully committed and attend each session so you can build trust and rapport with the other members.

- **Friendship:** The goal of any small group is to serve as a place where people can share, learn about God, and build friendships. So seek to make your group a "safe place." Be honest about your thoughts and feelings . . . but also listen carefully to everyone else's thoughts, feelings, and opinions. Keep anything personal that your group members share in confidence so that you can create a community where people can heal, be challenged, and grow spiritually.

If you are going through this study on your own, read the opening Welcome section and reflect on the questions in the Connect section. Watch the video and use the prompts provided to take notes. Finally, personalize the questions and exercises in the Discuss and Respond sections. Close by recording any requests you want to pray about during the week.

Personal Study

The personal study is for you to work through on your own during the week. Each exercise is designed to help you explore the key ideas you uncovered during your group time and delve into passages of Scripture that will help you apply those principles to your life. Go at your own pace, doing a little each day or all at once, and spend a few moments in silence to listen to what God might be saying to you. Each personal study will include:

- **Opening:** A brief introduction to lead you into the personal study for the day.
- **Scripture:** A few passages on the topic of the day for you to read and review.
- **Reflection:** Questions for you to answer related to the passages you just read.
- **Prayer:** A prompt to help you express what you've studied in a prayer to God.

If you are doing this study as part of a group, and you are unable to finish (or even start) these personal studies for the week, you should still attend the group time. Be assured that you are still wanted and welcome even if you don't have your "homework" done. The group studies and personal studies are intended to help you hear what God wants you to hear and how to apply what he is saying to your life. So . . . as you go through this study, be listening for him to speak to you as you learn about what it means to trust in the *God of the How and When.*

WEEK 1

BEFORE GROUP MEETING	Read the Introduction and Part 1 in *The God of the Way* Read the Welcome section (page 3)
GROUP MEETING	Discuss the Connect questions Watch the video teaching for session 1 Discuss the questions that follow as a group Do the closing exercise and pray (pages 3–14)
PERSONAL STUDY – DAY 1	Complete the daily study (pages 16–17)
PERSONAL STUDY – DAY 2	Complete the daily study (pages 19–20)
PERSONAL STUDY – DAY 3	Complete the daily study (pages 21–22)
PERSONAL STUDY – DAY 4	Complete the daily study (pages 23–24)
PERSONAL STUDY – DAY 5 (before week 2 group meeting)	Complete the daily study (pages 26–27) Read chapter 1 in *The God of the Way* Complete any unfinished personal studies

The Holy Land

GOD'S CHOSEN PLACE FOR HIS PEOPLE

"I am the LORD, the God of your father Abraham and the God of Isaac. I will give you and your descendants the land on which you are lying. Your descendants will be like the dust of the earth, and you will spread out to the west and to the east, to the north and to the south. All peoples on earth will be blessed through you and your offspring. I am with you and will watch over you wherever you go, and I will bring you back to this land. I will not leave you until I have done what I have promised you."

GENESIS 28:13–15

World of the Patriarchs

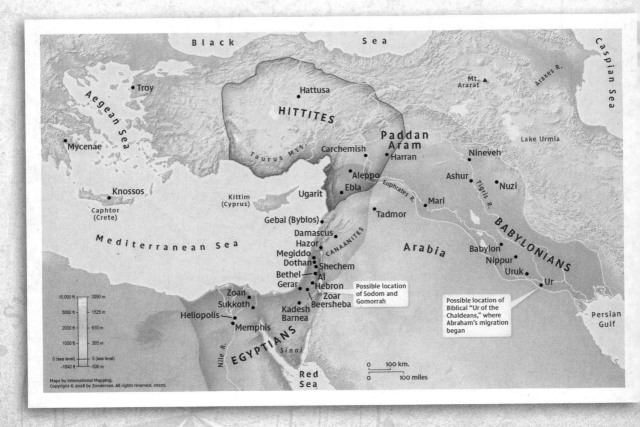

Black Sea

Caspian Sea

Aegean Sea

Troy

Hattusa

HITTITES

Mt. Ararat

Araxes R.

Lake Urmia

Mycenae

Taurus Mts.

Carchemish

Paddan Aram

Harran

Nineveh

Ashur

Tigris R.

Nuzi

Knossos

Aleppo

Ebla

Euphrates R.

Mari

Caphtor (Crete)

Kittim (Cyprus)

Ugarit

Tadmor

BABYLONIANS

Gebal (Byblos)

Mediterranean Sea

Damascus

CANAANITES

Arabia

Babylon

Nippur

Hazor

Megiddo

Dothan

Shechem

Uruk

Ur

Bethel

Ai

Gerar

Hebron

Zoar

Beersheba

Possible location of Sodom and Gomorrah

Possible location of Biblical "Ur of the Chaldeans," where Abraham's migration began

Zoan

Sukkoth

Kadesh Barnea

Persian Gulf

Heliopolis

Memphis

Nile R.

EGYPTIANS

Sinai

Red Sea

10,000 ft — 3050 m
5000 ft — 1525 m
2000 ft — 610 m
1000 ft — 305 m
0 (sea level) — 0 (sea level)
-1640 ft — -500 m

0   100 km.
0   100 miles

Maps by International Mapping.
Copyright © 2008 by Zondervan. All rights reserved. v0220.

Welcome | Read On Your Own

Welcome to the *God of the How and When*. Over the course of the next few weeks, you and your group will look at the stories of Abraham, Sarah, Moses, Jacob, and Mary (the mother of Jesus) in the Bible and examine why they are so important today. But before we start out on that journey, we first need to take a look at *where* these events will place. After all, every story needs a *setting* . . . and in God's story, this setting is Israel, or the "Holy Land."

We first learn of this place when the Lord calls Abraham to leave his hometown of Ur of the Chaldeans and travel to an undisclosed location that will be revealed to him. As the Lord instructs, "Go from your country, your people and your father's household to the land I will show you" (Genesis 12:1). Eventually, God leads Abraham to what is known in that time as Canaan. God promises to give this land to Abraham and his descendants and make him into a great nation. God even seals this promise with an agreement, or "covenant."

As the story of the Bible unfolds, we find that the God of the How and When—the one who determines *how* and *when* all things in Scripture will take place—is also concerned about *where* these things will take place. He reveals his plans and purposes in a specific location. But this should immediately raise some questions in our minds. *Why did God choose that particular piece of land? What is the significance of this place that we call Israel?*

In this opening session, you will learn the answer to those questions. You will discover the land of Israel had—and still has—both *geographic* and *spiritual* significance. You will learn about the type of agreement or "covenant" that God established with Abraham as it relates to this land and why it was so different from other covenants of the time. You will also follow the course of the promise that God made with Abraham to see how it played out in Israel's history.

It's going to be an exciting journey, so let's get started!

Connect | 15 minutes

If you or any of your group members don't know each other, take a few minutes to introduce yourselves. Then, to get things started, discuss one of the following questions:

- How would you describe your primary goal or hope for participating in this study? (In other words, why are you here?)

— *or* —

- How would you rate your ability to wait on God's timing? In what situations are you most tempted to rush ahead of his plans?

Watch | 20 minutes

Now it's time to watch the video for this session, which you can access by playing the DVD or through streaming (see the instructions provided on the inside front cover). As you watch, use the following outline to record any thoughts or concepts that stand out to you.

I. What is unique about Israel in the life of God's people?

   A. Spiritual significance

   1. The boundaries of the land that God promises to Abraham in the covenant are the same boundaries as the Garden of Eden.

   2. God was restoring everything lost in the Fall to the physical descendants of Abraham and also to the spiritual sons and daughters of Abraham.

   3. The rabbis say that the land of Israel is most fertile for producing prophets and people who hear God's voice in a unique way.

Geography of Israel

The land of Israel is located at the eastern coast of the Mediterranean Sea. It has been described by some as an area about the size of New Jersey with the geographical diversity of California. In a single day, a visitor can experience the heat of the desert in the south and then drive north to see the snow on the slopes of Mount Hermon. While there are many ways to describe the geography of Israel, five distinct regions can be easily identified.

The Coastal Plain. The coastal plain is located in the east of the country between the Mediterranean Sea and a hilly plateau at the center of Israel. It is about 140 miles in length and reaches from the southern edge of Lebanon to Gaza, gradually widening as it moves southward. Near its beginning in the north the coastal plain is interrupted by Mount Carmel.

The Central Hill Country. The entire central area of Israel is comprised of interlocking hills and plateaus, beginning in the north at an elevation of more than 3,000 feet. These hills are broken by the valley of Jezreel, but rise again into small hills in southern Galilee and Samaria. In the east, the Judean hills drop off sharply into the Rift Valley west of the Dead Sea.

The Rift Valley. The Rift Valley is located to the west of the Central Hill Country and slices like a great gash in the earth's crust through Palestine from north to south. This region runs the entire length of the Jordan River, beginning with its sources in the north, running to the Sea of Galilee, and meandering all the way down to the Dead Sea in the south.

The Transjordan Plateau. East of the Jordan River, rising sharply above the Rift Valley, is a high tableland known as the Transjordan Plateau. It can be subdivided into three main plateaus: the Bashan plateau in the north, the Moab and Gilead regions in the center, and the Sier mountain plateau in the south. Four major rivers or streams flow down into the Jordan River or Dead Sea from the plateau: the Yarmuk, the Jabbock, the Arnon, and the Zared.

The Desert. The Desert region (called the Negev) is located in the southern portion of Israel. It forms an inverted triangle shape whose western edge is contiguous with the desert of the Sinai Peninsula and whose eastern border is the Arabah valley. The Negev is a rocky and arid region interrupted by wadis (dry riverbeds that flow briefly after rain) and deep craters.[1]

B. Geographic significance

  1. The location of Israel was strategic because it served as a land bridge between the cultures that flourished in Africa and Asia.

  2. Significant trade routes such as the Via Maris ran through the land of Israel. There were key cities in Israel that protected these important trade routes.

II. What is the significance of God's covenant with Abraham as it relates to the land of Israel?

  A. Covenants in ancient times were more like what we would consider contracts.

  1. Both sides had stipulations to fulfill, and not fulfilling those stipulations would render the covenant null and void—and there were consequences for the side that broke it.

  2. Abraham was concerned that his descendants would ultimately not be faithful to follow God and would thus forfeit the promise the Lord was making to him.

B. God makes what is known as "the covenant between the parts."

   1. God tells Abraham to lay out sacrifices and causes a deep sleep to come over him. The Lord then passes through the parts of the sacrifices like a fiery torch and smoking oven.

   2. The sacrifices were symbolic of what would happen if the parties broke the terms. But only God passed through the parts, which meant this was an unconditional covenant.

   3. God's relationship with us is never conditional or contractual. His relationship with us is always formed on the basis of his grace and his goodness.

III. How did the covenant that God made with Abraham work out in Israel's history?

   A. God promises the land to Abraham, Isaac, and Jacob, and then ultimately raises up Moses to bring the children of Israel out of Egypt and into the Promised Land.

   1. Moses died in the desert because he lacked faith and disobeyed God. So the Lord raised up Joshua to bring the twelve tribes into the Promised Land.

Jerusalem at the Center of the World

In 1581, a German Protestant pastor published a map of the world that captures the ancient idea of Jerusalem being at the center of the world. The Bünting Clover Leaf Map, also known as The World in a Cloverleaf, depicts the world as a flower. The city of Jerusalem is seen at the center of the flower, with petals coming off that center that represent Europe, Asia, and Africa. Of course, Bünting understood that *geographically,* the world does not look like a flower with Jerusalem at its center. However, he wanted to show that *spiritually,* the city of Jerusalem—and what took place there—is at the center of everything that truly matters in this world. For it was in Jerusalem that Yeshua, the Messiah, "being found in appearance as a man . . . humbled himself by becoming obedient to death—even death on a cross!" (Philippians 2:8).

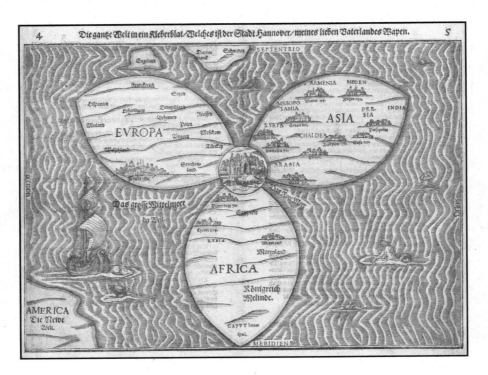

2. God ultimately raises up King David as the nation's second king. It is through King David that the people conquer the city of Jerusalem—the spiritual center of the world.

3. The house built for God (the Temple) is located on Mount Moriah, which is where God told Abraham to offer his son, Isaac, on the place that he would show to him.

4. The binding of Isaac ultimately points to the death of Yeshua, who is the greater than Isaac and the fulfillment of the promise made to Abraham.

B. Unfortunately, the Temple is destroyed because God's people are disobedient.

1. The rabbis state the First Temple was destroyed because the Israelites broke the First Commandment to "love the Lord your God." They committed *idolatry*.

2. The rabbis state the Second Temple was destroyed because the Israelites broke the Second Commandment to "love your neighbor." They engaged in *senseless hatred*.

3. The destruction of the Second Temple is tied to Israel's rejection of Yeshua. It is this temple, built by King Herod, over which Yeshua weeps.

IV. How does the land of Israel apply to us today?

   A. Israel is still at the center of God's plans and purposes for humanity.

   B. Just as the land of Israel was strategically located in ancient times, so the Lord is strategic in everything that he does in our lives.

   C. Just as the land of Israel was at the center of the world, so we need to make the Lord the center of our lives.

D. Looking to the land of Israel is looking to the Lord, and praying for the land is praying for the second coming. Jerusalem is going to be the eternal home for all believers in Yeshua.

Discuss | 35 minutes

Take some time to discuss what you just watched by answering the following questions. There are some suggested questions below to help you begin your discussion, but feel free to pick any of the additional questions as well as time allows.

Suggested Questions

1. God could have chosen any location on earth as the place to reveal his plans, purpose, and provisions to his people. Yet he chose the land of Israel as the setting for his great story. What was the spiritual significance of God choosing this land for his people?

2. The prophet Ezekiel wrote, "This is what the Sovereign LORD says: This is Jerusalem, which I have set in the center of the nations, with countries all around her" (Ezekiel 5:5). What was the geographical significance of God choosing Israel for his people?

3. Read Genesis 15:7–12. God appeared to Abraham and promised that he would give him the land of Canaan. However, Abraham was concerned that he and his descendants would violate the terms of God's covenant and thus forfeit the promise. How did God reassure Abraham in the way he conducted the "covenant between the parts"?

4. The place where God chose to build a house for himself was on Mount Moriah—the same place where God had told Abraham to offer his only son as a sacrifice. How does this location point to the greater sacrifice that would take place centuries later in Jerusalem when God's only Son entered into the world? Why is this significant?

Additional Questions

5. Read aloud 2 Chronicles 28:2–7. King David wanted to build the Temple, but the Lord determined that his son Solomon would be the one to construct it. The First Temple was completed around 950 BC but later destroyed in 587 BC by the Babylonians. But what do the rabbis say was the real reason why the First Temple was destroyed?

6. Read Haggai 2:9. God used Herod the Great in the first century AD to fulfill this prophecy. Herod enacted a large-scale renovation of the Second Temple that made it one of the wonders of the ancient world. This Temple was also destroyed, this time in AD 70 by the Romans. What do the rabbis say was the real reason for its destruction?

7. God strategically directed the events that led to Abraham and his descendants claiming the land of Israel, just as he strategically directs the events in your life today. God has a *reason* for everything he does—and he also has a *season* in which it takes place. What are some of the ways you have seen the truth of this statement play out in your life?

8. Just as Israel was the spiritual center of the ancient world, we need to make sure that God is the spiritual center of our world. What are some of the ways that you ensure God is always at the center? How has this had an impact on your life?

Respond | 10 minutes

Review the outline for the video teaching and any notes you took. In the space below, write down your most significant takeaway from this session.

Pray | 10 minutes

Praying for one another is one of the most important things you can do as a community. So use this time wisely and make it more than just a "closing prayer" to end your group experience. Be intentional about sharing your prayers, reviewing how God is answering your prayers, and actually praying for each other as a group. Use the space below to write down any requests so that you and your group members can continue to pray about them in the week ahead.

Name	Request

Personal Study

You are on a journey toward a better understanding of the God of the How and When. A key part of that growth, regardless of where you are spiritually, involves studying Scripture. This is the goal of these personal studies—to help you explore what the Bible has to say and how to apply God's Word to your life. As you work through each of these exercises, be sure to write down your responses to the questions, as you will be given a few minutes to share your insights at the start of the next session if you are doing this study with others. If you are reading *The God of the Way* alongside this study, first review the Introduction and Part 1 in the book.

— Day 1 —

More Than a Land

The Promised Land, the land of milk and honey, Canaan . . . the location had many names, but it was destined for one group of people. As the Bible unfolds, this land becomes a central character in the story of God and his people.[2] It is more than a strategically located territory. It is more than an agricultural epicenter. The land represents God's relationship with his people.

Land is a theme that runs throughout Scripture.[3] At the beginning of Genesis, Adam and Eve were exiled from the Garden of Eden—God's original gift of land—for their sin. A few chapters later, we learn about a new territory that God wanted to give his people through the patriarch Abraham (known as "Abram" before God changed his name). Abraham would have known Adam and Eve's story. He was all too aware of humankind's ability to sin. So, understandably, he was nervous when God wanted to enter into a covenant with him.

The reason for this is because the covenants of Abraham's day were always conditional (see "Ancient Covenants" on page 18). They were filled with warnings of the consequences that would occur if one of the parties broke the agreement. Abraham naturally assumed God would follow this same pattern in the covenant that he was making with him—and Abraham knew that neither he nor his descendants would be able to live up to the Lord's holy standards. However, God would set a new precedent with Abraham that would change the nature of covenants—and foreshadow the covenant that Jesus would make with all God's people.

In your group time this week, you read how Abraham questioned God about his promise to give the land of Canaan to him and his descendants (see Genesis 15:7–12). Today, you will read how this covenant (known as a *b'rit* in Hebrew) would be unique in that God *alone* would be responsible for fulfilling the terms.[4] He knew that Abraham would stray. He knew his ancestors certainly would stray. But his love would remain . . . and the land would be the proof. The people might be exiled, they might be enslaved, they might wander, but no matter what they did, God would bring them back to the land that he promised to Abraham.

Read | Genesis 15:12–21

Reflect

1. The "thick and dreadful darkness" that falls on Abraham after he has prepared the sacrifice (see verse 12) foreshadows the dark events that will occur in the lives of Abraham's future descendants. What does God say will happen to these descendants? How does God assure Abraham that he will see them through these troubles?

2. This prophecy from God, however, does not relate directly to Abraham. The Lord has a different future in mind for him. What does God say will happen to Abraham?

3. As you saw in this week's teaching, the land of Israel that God was giving to Abraham had both geographic and spiritual significance. What spiritual territory has God given you—whether that's an actual place, your family, or a community that you feel God has entrusted to you? How are you "taking possession" of that territory?

4. How have you experienced God's unconditional love in the context of this spiritual territory? How have you responded to God for this act of love to you?

Pray | End your time in prayer. Picture the territory God gave the Israelites, and then picture the territory God has given you. Ask God how you can be a good steward of this "land." Thank him for keeping his covenant with you.

Ancient Covenants

Several texts have survived that demonstrate the way in which sacrifices were used in forming covenants in ancient cultures between two parties. In each case, the destruction of the animal served as a representation of the consequences that would befall the party who violated the terms of the agreement. One example is a covenant from the eighth century BC between the Assyrian King Ashurnirari V and Aramean King Mati'ilu, which reads, in part:

> This spring lamb has been brought from its fold not for sacrifice, not for a banquet, not for a purchase . . . it has been brought to sanction the treaty between Ashurnirari and Mati'ilu. If Mati'ilu sins against (this) treaty made under oath by the gods, then, just as this spring lamb, brought from its fold, will not return to its fold. . . . Mati'ilu, together with his sons, daughters, officials, and the people of his land . . . will not return to his country, and not behold his country again. This head is not the head of a lamb, it is the head of Mati'ilu, it is the head of his sons, his officials, and the people of his land. If Mati'ilu sins against this treaty, so may, just as the head of this spring lamb is torn off . . . the head of Mati'ilu be torn off.[5]

Another example is a covenant from the seventh century BC, in which the Assyrian King Esarhaddon desired to secure the throne for his sons through a treaty with his vassals. The king first called on his Assyrian gods to strike down any parties who did not honor the agreement, saying, "If you sin against this treaty which [your] lord Esarhaddon, king of Assyria, has established with you . . . may Ashur, father of the gods, strike you down with his fierce weapons." The king then outlined the consequences for breaking the treaty, stating, among other curses, "Just as this ewe is cut open and the flesh of its young placed in its mouth, so may he . . . make you eat in your hunger the flesh of your brothers, your sons, and your daughters."[6]

Compare this language to words that God said to Abraham in his covenant—when the Lord himself passed between the two parts of the sacrifice: "To your descendants I give this land, from the Wadi of Egypt to the great river, the Euphrates—the land of the Kenites, Kenizzites, Kadmonites, Hittites, Perizzites, Rephaites, Amorites, Canaanites, Girgashites and Jebusites" (Genesis 15:18–21). No caustic remarks, conditions, or curses—just a commitment from the Lord God that he would fulfill his promise because he is merciful and faithful.

-Day 2-

Slavery

The covenant that God made with Abraham for the land of Israel was unconditional. However, just as the Lord said, Abraham's descendants eventually found themselves strangers in a country that was not their own. During the time of Jacob, they journeyed to Egypt to escape a famine in Canaan. There they settled in Goshen and multiplied greatly (see Genesis 42:1–2; 46:1–7, 28–29; Exodus 1:6–7). But this concerned a king of Egypt, who worried they might join with their enemies if a war broke out. So he put them all into slavery (see Exodus 1:8–11).

You will learn more about the Israelites' deliverance under Moses in a future session, but for now imagine what it would be like to be one of the Hebrews born into slavery. All you've known is captivity. All your *parents* have known is captivity . . . and their parents before them. Your people have been enslaved for *400 years*. You've heard the story of Abraham and the covenant that God made with him. But it is difficult for you to imagine your people ever owning such prized territory when all you and those before you have known is bondage.

All God's people have known this type of captivity and yearning for freedom. When Jesus came, he came to an enslaved people. Perhaps they weren't literally enslaved—though, of course, slavery has continued throughout the generations. But they were slaves to their sin. Stuck, trapped, and unable to imagine freedom. Jesus came to reclaim what was lost. Through his sacrifice and the New Covenant, he freed us from sin. And because of this freedom, we can reclaim our lives, our hearts, and our souls as *our* territory and not the enemy's.

Read | Exodus 1:8–14 and Galatians 4:1–7

Reflect

1. Joseph had risen to a position of second-in-command during his time in Egypt. He had been instrumental in helping the Egyptians navigate a famine that stretched across the entire region (see Genesis 41:41–57). But according to the account from

Exodus, after Joseph's death, a king came to power in Egypt who knew nothing of what Joseph had done. What actions did this new king take against the Israelites?

2. The apostle Paul saw all of humanity in a similar plight. According to his words in Galatians, what status did we hold before the arrival of Christ? What status does God now offer to us because of the sacrifice made by his only Son?

3. What does this passage in Galatians reveal about the way that God views you? Where have you experienced freedom from bondage in your life because of Christ?

4. Where do you need still need to experience this freedom in your life—a place where sin or shame is still holding you back? Explain.

Pray | Focus on the last question during your prayer time. Name the sin or shame that is keeping you in bondage. Ask Jesus for radical freedom. If you're struggling with believing that freedom is possible, speak honestly about that with the Father.

Day 3

Wilderness

The 400 years of captivity for the Israelites ended with a great exodus from Egypt. Under the leadership of Moses, the Lord guided the people out of the region of Goshen and instructed them to head toward Canaan—the "promised land" that had been given to Abraham. The Pharaoh soon regretted his decision to allow his slave labor force to go free and sent his chariots to return the people back to Egypt. But God parted the waters of the Red Sea, allowing the Israelites to escape on dry land, and then closed the waves down on their pursuers.

After this miraculous escape, the Israelites hoped they would soon be back in the Promised Land. Unfortunately, when they reached the border, a report from ten spies who had been sent to investigate the land caused the people to doubt the faithfulness of God and his power to lead them to victory over the inhabitants. As a result, God decreed the Israelites would wander in the wilderness for not a few days, weeks, or months . . . but *forty years*.

Now, instead of finding themselves in the land of milk and honey, the Israelites found themselves in a land of desolation. Perhaps you found yourself in a similar place in your life—seasons when your work, pursuits, and relationships felt fruitless. The wilderness can feel like a stagnant place . . . an arid and inhospitable desert where nothing can flourish. But in Scripture, we find that the wilderness can actually represent a time of transition or liminal space—"an in-between place where ordinary life is suspended, identity shifts, and new possibilities emerge."[7] In the wilderness, the Israelites were forged together as God's people again.

Jesus likewise found himself in the wilderness during a time of transition. Right before he began his public ministry, he was led into the wilderness by the Holy Spirit, where he was tempted by Satan. Jesus was being tested. Who was he? Was he going to be able to deliver God's people to salvation as Moses had delivered the Israelites out of Egypt? It was in the desert that Jesus showed Satan what he was up against: the Son of the one true God.[8]

So don't discount the wilderness times in your life. Lean into the work that God wants to do there. Who you are and who God is making you to be happens in the wilderness.

Read | Numbers 21:4–9 and Matthew 4:1–10

Reflect

1. The Israelites' wilderness wandering takes place after they had rebelled against God at Kadesh and been prohibited from entering the Promised Land. How did the Israelites feel about being in the desert? How did God respond to their grumbling?

2. The story of Jesus' time in the wilderness takes place immediately after he is baptized in the Jordan River and right before he preaches his first recorded sermon in Nazareth (see Matthew 3:13–17; 4:12–17). What did this time in the wilderness represent for Christ?

3. When have you been led into the wilderness—a time of spiritual, relational, or personal drought? How did you feel about being in this place at first?

4. What did you learn about yourself during this wilderness time in your life? What did you learn about the love and faithfulness of God?

Pray | If you find yourself in the wilderness today, ask God why you're here. Listen and see what he has to teach you. If you are out of the wilderness, thank God for delivering you. Reflect on who you became as a result of that season.

-Day 4-

Exile

Under the leadership of Joshua, whom you will learn about in a future session, the Israelites finally entered into the Promised Land. But Israel's relationship with God and, therefore, their relationship with the land that he gave to them, would be tumultuous. Several hundred years after the Israelites took possession of the land, Israel was divided into two kingdoms: the northern kingdom of Israel, and the southern kingdom of Judah.

The prophets Hosea and Isaiah warned that Judah and Israel, as a result of their disobedience to the Lord, would be conquered by foreign powers (see Hosea 9; Isaiah 39). The fall of Israel was completed in 721 BC, when the Assyrians completed their invasion and forcibly resettled the people in other lands. The fall of Judah was completed by 586 BC, when the Babylonians besieged Jerusalem and destroyed it. The people of Judah were also taken as captives to other lands (see "The Return to Jerusalem" on page 25).

The Israelites—as a result of their unfaithfulness to God—had once again been forced to live as captives and foreigners in a strange land. This was devastating to God's people, who had been living in the Promised Land for generations. Being away from home is difficult enough. But not knowing if you will ever return? It was heartbreaking.

Have you ever been in exile—far from home, in a foreign place, unsure of what is expected of you? You don't have to go far to feel this way. You can move to the next town over and feel like a stranger in a strange land. You can feel like a stranger in your own home. The feeling of exile is isolating and lonely. All you want is a place where you can feel at home, seen, and loved. God's people knew this feeling well, and as you'll read in the following psalm, they lamented their exile and kept Jerusalem close to their hearts.

Read | Psalm 137:1–6

Reflect

1. The author of this psalm reflects on the time when the people lived by "the rivers of Babylon" and hung their harps "on the poplars" (verses 1–2). Life had been good for

many of the captives when it came to material benefits. Yet while Babylon may have been a pleasant country, the people of Judah recognized they were aliens in a foreign land. Based on the tone of this psalm, how do you think the psalmist was feeling?

2. The author of this psalm writes that the Babylonian captors ("our tormentors") demanded the people of Judah to "sing songs of joy" (verse 3). How does the psalmist respond to this request? Why do you think it was so important for him and the other Jewish people to remember Jerusalem?

3. As noted previously, you don't have to go far to feel like an exile. You can even feel like a stranger in your own home. When is a time in your life that you have been in exile—a time when you have felt like a foreigner in a foreign land?

4. What feelings or sentiments from this psalm particularly resonate with you? What is the value of remembering "where you came from" when you find yourself in exile?

Pray | End your time in prayer. Remember that no matter where you are, God sees you. You are always known and loved by him. Meditate on that truth.

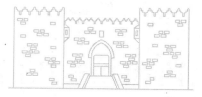

The Return to Jerusalem

The Babylonians occupied Judah beginning in 597 BC. The Bible states that when Zedekiah, the last king of Judah, rebelled against the king, the Babylonians marched on Jerusalem and destroyed the city in 586 BC (see 2 Kings 25). The people of Judah were taken into exile in Babylon and other places in the empire. But in 539 BC, the Persian king Cyrus the Great invaded the Babylon Empire and conquered it. Cyrus instituted a policy that allowed captive peoples to return to their homelands, which encouraged the Jews to start returning to the land of Palestine in three primary waves.

The First Wave. Shortly after Cyrus issued his decree, a man named Zerubbabel led the first group of exiles back to their homeland, sometime between 538–520 BC. Zerubbabel was a descendant of King David (see Matthew 1:6, 12) and led 42,360 people back to Judah, accompanied by 7,337 slaves and 200 singers (see Ezra 2:64–65). Zerubbabel also laid the foundation for building the Second Temple in Jerusalem soon after (see 3:8; 5:2).

The Second Wave. The second wave of exiles was led by a priest and scribe named Ezra sometime around 458 BC (see Ezra 7:6). Ezra carried a letter from the Persian king Artaxerxes I that authorized any Jewish person to travel back to Jerusalem with him (see verses 12–26). However, only around 1,754 males responded—and none of the Levites answered the call (see 8:1–15). When Ezra arrived in Jerusalem, he found that many had violated the law concerning mixed marriages (see 9:1–2). Ezra ultimately led the people to repentance (see 10:1–17).

The Third Wave. The third wave of exiles was led by Nehemiah, a cupbearer to king Artaxerxes I, who was granted permission to return to Jerusalem and rebuild its walls (see Nehemiah 2:5–8). Nehemiah faced challenges from enemies, but the wall was nevertheless finished in only fifty-two days (see 6:15). Nehemiah, with the help of Ezra and, later, the prophet Malachi, encouraged various spiritual reforms in Judah (see 13:1–31)

- Day 5 -

Our Promised Land

The Israelites were ultimately delivered from exile during the rule of the Persian king Cyrus the Great. However, in 63 BC, Pompey the Great claimed the city of Jerusalem for Rome. The glory days of the Israelites were long gone, and the Jews were now living as an oppressed minority in the land promised to Abraham and their ancestors.

However, over the centuries, the prophets foretold of a coming Messiah. Isaiah had written, "In that day the Root of Jesse will stand as a banner for the peoples; the nations will rally to him, and his resting place will be glorious" (11:10). By the time of Christ, the people were expecting the Messiah to be a great political leader, descended from the line of King David, who would overthrow Rome and return Israel to its former glory.

But Jesus had a bigger kingdom in mind—the kingdom of God that stretched far beyond the borders of ancient Palestine and into the entire world. Instead of seeking empirical glory, "he [chose] to live without a home going around teaching others what relationship with God is all about."[9] A relationship with God *made possible through him*.

In the New Covenant, Jesus reclaimed our hearts for himself, and he asked us to do the same. His final command to his disciples, known as the Great Commission, was to increase God's kingdom by telling the nations about him.[10] In this way, he invited *all* into Abraham's Promised Land, no longer reserved for the Israelites but for all God's people, creating the kingdom of God on earth while we wait to enter the kingdom of God for eternity.

Read | Matthew 28:16–20 and Acts 1:7–11

Reflect

1. Jesus gives the same commission to all of his followers, regardless of whether they worship him or doubt. What does this say about the way that Christ can use you for God's kingdom—even if you have doubts?

2. Jesus reveals that "all authority in heaven and on earth" has been given to him. What instructions does Jesus then give in Matthew 28:19–20? What other promises does Jesus give to his followers before he is taken into heaven (see Acts 1:8)?

3. What does the Great Commission look like in your life? What are some of the ways that you are sharing Jesus' love and message with those around you?

4. The land of Israel is the place where God's people have always placed their hope. It's the place to which Jesus came, it is where he died, it is where he ascended into heaven, and ultimately it is going to be the place where he places his feet at the second coming (see Zechariah 14:3–4). So, looking to the land of Israel—the "Holy Land"—is looking for his return. As you conclude this study, how is that truth impacting your day-to-day life?

Pray | Spend a few minutes reflecting on this week's personal study time. Did God convict you of anything this week? Did you change in any way or learn something new? Talk to God about what you discovered in his Word this week and what he might be showing you today.

For Next Week

Before you meet again with your group next week, read chapter 1 in *The God of the Way*. Also go back and complete any of the study and reflection questions from this personal study that you weren't able to finish.

WEEK 2

BEFORE GROUP MEETING	Read chapter 1 in *The God of the Way* Read the Welcome section (page 31)
GROUP MEETING	Discuss the Connect questions Watch the video teaching for session 2 Discuss the questions that follow as a group Do the closing exercise and pray (pages 31–42)
PERSONAL STUDY – DAY 1	Complete the daily study (pages 44–45)
PERSONAL STUDY – DAY 2	Complete the daily study (pages 46–47)
PERSONAL STUDY – DAY 3	Complete the daily study (pages 48–49)
PERSONAL STUDY – DAY 4	Complete the daily study (pages 50–51)
PERSONAL STUDY – DAY 5 (before week 3 group meeting)	Complete the daily study (pages 52–53) Read chapter 2 in *The God of the Way* Complete any unfinished personal studies

Abraham

GOD'S PERFECT TIMING

[Abraham] said, "Sovereign LORD, what can you give me since I remain childless and the one who will inherit my estate is Eliezer of Damascus? . . . You have given me no children; so a servant in my household will be my heir." Then the word of the LORD came to him: "This man will not be your heir, but a son who is your own flesh and blood will be your heir. . . . Look up at the sky and count the stars— if indeed you can count them. . . . So shall your offspring be."

GENESIS 15:2–5

Abraham's Journey

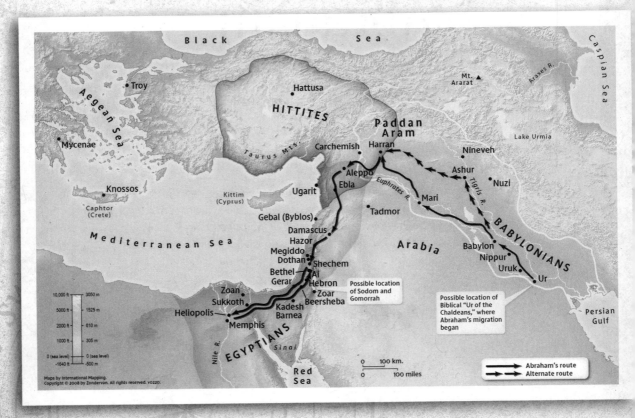

Black Sea

Caspian Sea

Aegean Sea

Troy

Hattusa

HITTITES

Mt. Ararat

Araxes R.

Paddan Aram

Lake Urmia

Carchemish

Harran

Nineveh

Mycenae

Taurus Mts.

Aleppo

Ashur

Nuzi

Ebla

Euphrates R.

Knossos

Kittim (Cyprus)

Ugarit

Tigris R.

Mari

BABYLONIANS

Caphtor (Crete)

Gebal (Byblos)

Tadmor

Damascus

Mediterranean Sea

Hazor

Arabia

Babylon

Megiddo

Dothan

Shechem

Nippur

Uruk

Bethel

Ai

Ur

Gerar

Hebron

Zoan

Zoar

Beersheba

Possible location of Sodom and Gomorrah

Sukkoth

Kadesh Barnea

Heliopolis

Possible location of Biblical "Ur of the Chaldeans," where Abraham's migration began

Persian Gulf

Memphis

EGYPTIANS

Nile R.

Sinai

Red Sea

10,000 ft   3050 m
5000 ft   1525 m
2000 ft   610 m
1000 ft   305 m
0 (sea level) 0 (sea level)
-1640 ft   -500 m

0   100 km.
0   100 miles

Abraham's route
Alternate route

Maps by International Mapping.
Copyright © 2008 by Zondervan. All rights reserved. Y0220.

Welcome | Read On Your Own

In the last session, you looked at the covenant that God made with Abraham as it related to giving the land of Israel to him and his descendants. You saw that the Lord—following the practices in the culture of the day—initiated what is known as "the covenant between the parts" (see Genesis 15:9–21). However, it was only *God* who passed through the parts of the sacrifice, indicating that his covenant with Abraham was to be unilateral and unconditional.

Yet giving the land of Israel to Abraham was only part of the covenant. God also promised to make Abraham "into a great nation" (12:2). He told Abraham that he would make his offspring as numerous as "the dust of the earth" (13:16). He led Abraham out into the night as said, "Look up at the sky and count the stars—if indeed you can count them. . . . So shall your offspring be" (15:5). God's promises were clear. He would make Abraham's descendants into a great nation and provide the land of Israel as their home.

There was just one major problem for Abraham. He and his wife, Sarah, were childless. What's more, Abraham was *seventy-five years old* when God first made this promise to him (see 12:4), and Sarah was around *sixty-five years of age*! By all accounts, the couple was well past the normal childbearing years, so it was hard for them to see *how* God would make this promise of an heir come to pass. Even worse, God did not say *when* this promise would be fulfilled. As the years passed by, and Abraham and Sarah grew older, and still no child came, their faith dwindled that God would ever fulfill this promise.

In this session, you will look at both the *physical* and *spiritual* components of this covenant that God made with Abraham. You will continue ahead in Abraham's story and learn what he and Sarah did to "help out" God in making this promise of a son come to pass—and the consequences that resulted when they moved ahead of the Lord's timing. You will see why God changed his name to Abraham and the significance of that new name. You will also explore the story of how God, once the promised son was born, instructed Abraham to sacrifice his only son on Mount Moriah—and how this event points to the greater sacrifice of God's only Son.

Connect | 15 minutes

Welcome to session 2 of *The God of the How and When.* If you or any of your group members are not yet acquainted, take a few minutes to introduce yourselves. Then, to get things started, discuss one of the following questions:

- What is a key insight or takeaway from last week's personal study that you would like to share with the group?

— *or* —

- When is a time in your life that God proved his faithfulness to you? How did God coming through in that situation draw you closer to him?

Watch | 20 minutes

Now watch the video for this session (remember that you can access this video via streaming by following the instructions printed on the inside front cover). As you watch, use the following outline to record any thoughts or concepts that stand out to you.

I. What was involved in God's call to Abraham to leave his homeland?

A. Abraham's call from God occurs in two stages.

1. God first calls Abraham to leave his homeland in Ur of the Chaldeans and travel about 600 miles to a place called Harran (see Genesis 11:31).

2. God then calls Abraham to leave Harran and go to a place that he did not know, which ultimately turns out to be the Promised Land (see Genesis 12:1).

B. God rewards Abraham for being willing to go without knowing the *how* or the *when*.

1. God rewards Abraham *physically*.

a. God promises Abraham that he will have descendants like "the stars in the sky" and "the sand on the seashore" (Genesis 22:17).

    b. Sand is indestructible. Part of God's promise to Abraham is that the Jewish people would never be destroyed.

    c. Sand is also the primary building block in the construction of concrete. The descendants of Abraham would be the building blocks for the kingdom of God.

2. God rewards Abraham spiritually.

    a. God establishes a unique relationship with Abraham. Abraham hears the voice of the Lord and has encounters with him (see Genesis 12:7).

    b. God says the nations of the world would be blessed through Abraham's descendants (see Genesis 12:3). God wanted the biological children of Abraham to be a source of blessing to the world.

C. Abraham did not always operate in God's timing.

1. Abraham went through many tests. The first was to leave everything he knew, but a greater test was to believe God's promise that he would have children in old age.

Abraham's Travels

Most scholars today believe that Abraham's hometown of Ur was located near the modern-day city of Nasiriyah in southern Iraq. If this is the true location, it means that Abraham and his family would have traveled more than 600 miles from Ur to Haran and another 400 or more miles from Haran to Shechem in Canaan. Here is where that journey would have taken him.

In Abraham's day, the only practical way to travel from Ur to Canaan was to follow a route that ran through a region known as the Fertile Crescent—an arc of fertile land where crops flourished and civilization thrived. Numerous cities were located along the banks of the Euphrates and Tigris rivers, and Abraham would have likely journeyed on established routes complete with milestones, patrols, river fords, guardhouses, food depots, and secure cities.

Abraham's first important stop would have been the city of Babylon, protected in that time by walls with nine gates. It was home to the Temple of Marduk and the Eteme-an-ki ziggurat, which rose to a height of nearly 300 feet. From there, it is possible that Abraham stopped beyond a wide curve of the Tigris River at a village called Baghdad, insignificant in his day, and then journeyed north to Ashur, a city dedicated to the worship of the god Ashur and goddess Ishtar. If Abraham followed this route, he would have stopped in Nineveh to replenish his supplies before setting out on the most strenuous part of the journey.

If Abraham followed a more westerly route along the Euphrates River, he would have likely stopped in the city of Mari, which flourished as a center of trade in the region. The city was designed as two concentric rings, with the outer ring protecting the city from floods and the inner ring protecting it from invaders. Regardless of the route Abraham took, the Bible states that he then ended up in Harran, located in the region of Paddan Aram.

From Harran, Abraham would have likely traveled through the Beqaa Valley, a fertile strip of land in modern-day Lebanon, before proceeding to the city of Aleppo. It is possible he then went through Ebla, one of the earliest kingdoms in Syria, before stopping in Damascus, one of the oldest continually inhabited cities on earth. From there, Abraham would have traveled south along the bank of the Jordan River, possibly through the fortified city of Hazor, before reaching Shechem in the land of Canaan. It was there the Lord appeared to Abraham and said, "To your offspring I will give this land" (Genesis 12:7).[11]

2. At one point, Abraham and Sarah took matters into their own hands. They went to their handmaid Hagar, and she conceived and had Ishmael (see Genesis 16:1–4).

3. If we wait for the Lord, we will never be left wanting. This is the promise we find in Isaiah: "Those who hope in the LORD will renew their strength . . . they will run and not grow weary, they will walk and not be faint" (Isaiah 40:31).

II. Why did God change Abraham and Sarah's names?

A. God adds one Hebrew letter to their names—the letter is *hei*.

1. *Hei* is the letter of the divine breath (see Psalm 33:6).

2. There was no way in the natural that Abraham and Sarah could conceive, so God adds the supernatural power and potential that gives them the ability to bear children.

B. God wants to take us from barrenness to birthing.

1. In Jewish tradition, the day Sarah conceives is the Feast of Trumpets. On that day, the people celebrate by blowing the *shofar* (a ram's horn; see Leviticus 23:24–25).

2. The sound of the shofar is made through the breath—the *hei*. It's the breath of the mouth that produces the sound of the *shofar*.

3. So the day that Sarah conceives represents the divine breath of God working to bring about his promise and his plans in her and Abraham's lives.

III. Why does God then ask Abraham to sacrifice his only son?

A. God's instruction to Abraham was to "go."

1. When God first calls Abraham to leave everything—the first test—his words begin with the Hebrew phrase *Lech lecha,* which means "go" (see Genesis 12:1).

2. When God calls Abraham to sacrifice Isaac—the last test—his words also begin with that Hebrew phrase *Lech lecha* (see Genesis 22:2).

B. What God was saying to Abraham through his instruction to "go."

1. In the first test, God was saying to Abraham, "Will you trust me with your past? Will you leave your family, your homeland, and everything that's familiar behind?"

The Shofar and Feast of Trumpets

"Say to the Israelites: 'On the first day of the seventh month you are to have a day of sabbath rest, a sacred assembly commemorated with trumpet blasts. Do no regular work, but present a food offering to the LORD'" (Leviticus 23:24–25).

This passage from the book of Leviticus describes a festival known as the Feast of Trumpets. At the time this feast was ordained, the Israelites had been brought out of Egypt under Moses and received the covenant at Mount Sinai. The people had witnessed God deliver them from the might of the Egyptian army through the ten plagues. They had seen God provide food and water for them in the wilderness. They had experienced God leading them in a pillar of cloud by day and a pillar of fire by night and had overcome their enemies.

The people had seen God do many miraculous things on their behalf, but unfortunately, they had very short memories of these great deeds. So the Lord established the Feast of Trumpets (and other festivals in the Hebrew calendar) as a time for them to do no work but simply reflect and remember what God had done. In addition, the people were to present a food offering to the Lord, as described in Numbers 29:1–6:

> On the first day of the seventh month hold a sacred assembly and do no regular work. It is a day for you to sound the trumpets. As an aroma pleasing to the LORD, offer a burnt offering of one young bull, one ram and seven male lambs a year old, all without defect. . . . They are food offerings presented to the LORD, a pleasing aroma.

The Feast of Trumpets was announced with a "trumpet blast." The instrument employed for this purpose was a *shofar,* which was typically made from a ram's horn. Unlike our modern trumpets, the shofar lacked any pitch-altering devices, so the sound and intensity of the blast were dependent on the person blowing into it. In addition to the Feast of Trumpets, the shofar was used to announce the new moon (see Psalm 81:3), the year of Jubilee (see Leviticus 25:9), at the start of a war (see Joshua 6:4), and in processions (see 2 Samuel 6:14–15).[12]

    2. In the last test, God was saying to Abraham, "Okay, you've trusted me with your past, but will you trust me with the promise of your future?"

    3. Isaac is a portrait and a picture of God giving his only begotten Son, the Lamb of God, on that same mountain as a sacrifice for us.

  C. When Abraham is about to offer Isaac, he looks up and sees a ram caught in a thicket.

    1. Abraham names that place Adonai Yireh, "The LORD Will Provide" (Genesis 22:14).

    2. Just like God provided for Abraham, he wants us to trust in him for provision, because the Lord always has a ram in the bush.

IV. What can we take from Abraham's story and apply to our lives today?

  A. We have to be willing to move forward without knowing all the details. God doesn't tell us everything about the how and when, but he calls us to step out in faith and trust him.

B. We can have *shalom*—the peace of God—in the midst of our struggles. Abraham and Sarah maintained their peace even when they didn't have all the details of the future.

C. Abraham and Sarah model what it looks like to walk in the *shalom* of God. We have to trust in the Lord and realize that we never have to go it alone, for he is always with us.

Discuss | 35 minutes

Take some time to discuss what you just watched by answering the following questions. There are some suggested questions below to help you begin your discussion, but feel free to pick any of the additional questions as well as time allows.

Suggested Questions

1. God rewarded Abraham *physically* when he was obedient to leave his homeland and travel to a place the Lord would ultimately reveal to him. The Lord promised to give Abraham land and make his descendants as numerous as "the sand on the seashore" (Genesis 22:17). What were some of the *spiritual* rewards that Abraham received?

2. Abraham went through tests. The first was to leave his homeland in Ur of the Chaldeans and journey to Canaan. But a greater test was to believe God's promise that he and Sarah would have children in old age. What are some of the ways that Abraham tried to rush God's timing? Why do you think it was so difficult for him to wait?

3. Read Genesis 22:1–5. Abraham's final test occurred after Isaac was born (and was likely in his thirties). The Lord instructed Abraham to take his only son and sacrifice him as a burnt offering on Mount Moriah. How did Abraham respond to this command? What does Abraham's response reveal about his complete trust in God?

4. Read 1 John 4:7–12. When Abraham was about to sacrifice his son on Mount Moriah, the Lord stayed his hand and provided a ram caught in a thicket as a substitute. However, in this passage, we see that God was willing to go through with the sacrifice of offering up his one and only Son for our sins. What does John say our response should be to this act of love? How easy is it for you to follow this command?

Additional Questions

5. The name *Abram* in Hebrew means "exalted father." When God added the Hebrew letter *hei* to his name, making it *Abraham,* it changed the meaning to "father of many."

The Hebrew letter *hei* is the letter of "divine breath." So what was God saying to Abraham about his divine power by adding this letter to his name?

6. Read John 10:7–10. The story of Abraham and Sarah reveals that God was to take us from barrenness to birthing. He wants to give us "life to the full." What are some ways you have witnessed God taking you from spiritual barrenness to birthing something brand new in you? How would you describe what it means to have "life to the full"?

7. Abraham and Sarah were willing to move forward when God called them to act without knowing all the details. While they weren't perfect people by any means, and while they stumbled at times, they are regarded as heroes of the faith for their willingness to take risks for God and trust that he would work it out in the end. What have you learned from their story that you can apply to your walk of faith with God?

8. Read Philippians 4:8–9. Another lesson that we can learn from Abraham and Sarah's story is that we can have *shalom*—the peace of God—in the midst of our trials. How did Abraham and Sarah demonstrate that they had this peace? What is one area in your life right now where you especially need God's *shalom*?

Respond | 10 minutes

Review the outline for the video teaching and any notes you took. In the space below, write down your most significant takeaway from this session.

Pray | 10 minutes

End your time by praying together as a group, asking the Lord to help you learn to better wait on his timing. Ask if anyone has any prayer requests to share. Write those requests in the space below so you and your group members can pray about them in the week ahead.

Name   Request

Personal Study

As you discussed in your group time this week, when God calls you to step out in faith, he won't always reveal the details of how you will get there or when it will happen. However, like Abraham, when you choose to follow his path in spite of all the obstacles you see along the way, he will reward your faith and provide for you in ways you never believed possible. When you are walking with God, you never need to fear that you will get lost along the way. As you explore these themes in the life of Abraham this week, be sure to write down your responses to the questions in the spaces provided, as you will be given a few minutes to share your insights at the start of the next session if you are doing this study with others. If you are reading *The God of the Way* alongside this study, first review chapter 1 in the book.

Day 1

When God Says Go

Our first encounter with Abraham is a story of obedience. God calls him to leave his country, his people, and his father's household. While leaving our parents' household today is common and expected, in Abraham's time, this departure signified a great loss. Ancient societies depended on territory, family, and inheriting the family land as a means for survival, so when Abraham left his father's household, he was also leaving behind his identity, his future, and his security.[13]

Perhaps you can relate. Maybe at some point in the past you have left your home, your family, and everything familiar that you've known to strike out into the unknown. If so, you can understand how Abraham and his family might have been feeling. Afraid, scared, uncertain, nervous about the future. Maybe you also understand a bit of the ache of the loss he felt . . . the grief and sadness of leaving behind everything that you love.

It is important to remember that *God* called Abraham to do this. He asked Abraham to step into the unknown—and it wouldn't be the last time that he would call Abraham to make a sacrifice. But the Lord also made a promise to Abraham. Leaving his family and inheritance behind had a point and a purpose. God was about to raise up a new nation to whom he would reveal his will and his ways, and he wanted Abraham to leave behind all the gods and religious practices that were so prevalent in his homeland of Ur of the Chaldeans.

As the psalmist wrote, "As for God, his way is perfect: the LORD's word is flawless; he shields all who take refuge in him" (Psalm 18:30). Abraham didn't always understand *how* and *when* God would lead him along his way. But he always trusted God's way was perfect.

Read | Genesis 12:1–7

Reflect

1. As previously noted, God's promise to Abraham included both a promise of land and a promise of descendants. The land promise is referenced in verse 1. What is included

in God's promise of descendants in verses 2–3? What is God's intention for Abraham's descendants as it relates to the people groups and nations of the world?

2. Abraham responded to God's call by packing up his belongings and setting out for the land of Canaan. The Bible states that he was accompanied on this journey by his wife, Sarah, his nephew Lot, and all the family's servants and people "they had acquired in Harran" (verse 5). What happened once Abraham reached the town of Shechem?

3. When have you "packed up your belongings" and stepped into the unknown as Abraham did—whether that was a move, a job change, or joining a new community? How did that transition feel? What helped you to adapt to your new surroundings?

4. What about right now? Do you feel God calling you to go, as he called Abraham, into an unknown territory in your life? If so, how are your responding to that call?

Pray | Spend a few moments in prayer. If you feel that God is calling you to step into a new area of your life, much like he called Abraham, ask him to give you the courage to go where he is calling you and the peace and assurance that he will be with you on the journey.

Day 2

A Promise Delayed

Abraham was established as the founder of God's new nation much later in life at age seventy-five. God had promised Abraham, "I will make you into a great nation" (Genesis 12:2). But this promise was not fulfilled immediately. In fact, twenty-five years passed between God's revelation of this promise to Abraham and Sarah and its fulfilment. Abraham had to wait patiently . . . which he didn't always do well.

We first get a glimpse of Abraham's doubts and, perhaps, a bit of his impatience in Genesis 15:1–21, when the Lord appears to him in a vision and reaffirms his promise to make Abraham into a great nation. By this time, Abraham has left his homeland and travelled to Canaan (see 12:1–9), spent some time in Egypt (see 12:10–20), parted ways with his nephew Lot (see 13:1–18), and rescued that same nephew (see 14:1–24). As one commentator notes, up until this point God has spoken to Abraham, but not the other way around.[14]

Now Abraham speaks to God and asks some questions. He wants to know if a servant in his household can serve as his heir. God reiterates that Abraham will have an heir of his "own flesh and blood" (15:4). So Abraham abandons the idea of placing a servant in this role. However, as you will read in today's passage, his impatience leads him to try and manipulate God's promise of a "flesh and blood" heir in a different way.

You have probably approached God with questions before, especially when you were waiting on something. *God, will this ever happen? Are you still faithful to me? Are you still good?* Abraham's story reveals that God's answer to these questions is *yes*. Even more, he remains faithful and good when we try to rush ahead of his perfect plans.

Read | Genesis 16:1–16

Reflect

1. The first section of this passage focuses on Sarah's plan to overcome her barrenness by having Hagar, her Egyptian slave, bear an heir for Abraham. However, it is

apparent that Abraham is a willing participant in this plan. How long does the text say that Abraham and Sarah had waited for a son at this point? How do you think that delay played into their desire to "move things along" in God's promise to them?

2. Abraham and Sarah's plan resulted in Hagar bearing a child. However, things immediately began to go awry after the child was born, for Hagar started to look down on Sarah for being unable to conceive. How did Sarah respond to this turn of events?

3. God did not leave Hagar and her newborn son to die in the desert. Instead, the Lord met her and gave her the promise that her descendants would also become a nation. How did Hagar respond after she heard these words from God?

4. The prophecy concerning Ishmael was that he would be "a wild donkey of a man" and that he would "live in hostility toward all his brothers" (verse 12). In the end, Abraham and Sarah's plan to rush ahead of God's timing resulted in only strife. How have you seen this same principle play out in your life or the life of a loved one?

Pray | Spend a few minutes in prayer. If you're still waiting on a promise from God or a desire of your heart to be fulfilled, bring that before the Lord and ask him to give you patience in this season of waiting. Be honest with him about how you feel. Ask him to restore your hope as you wait.

Hagar in the New Testament.
The apostle Paul would later use the story of Hagar in his letter to the Galatians to explain the difference between law and grace. Paul writes that Hagar and Sarah represent two covenants. Hagar, "the slave woman," stands for the covenant made at Mount Sinai (the law). Sarah, "the free woman," stands for the covenant made by the Messiah in Jerusalem (God's grace). Paul's implication is that those who adhere to the covenant of "the slave woman" are kept in slavery, while those who adhere to the covenant of "the free women" are set free. He concludes that "we are not children of the slave woman, but of the free woman" (see Galatians 4:21–31).

Day 3

A New Identity

As we've noted in this study, when we first encounter Abraham, he is actually not called "Abraham." Instead, the Bible states that his given name is "Abram." Hebrew names have meaning in Scripture, and the name Abram means "exalted father." In some ways, this seems like a fitting name for the man who would one day be the patriarch of the Israelite nation. He indeed is seen to this day as the "exalted father" of the Jewish people.

But God wanted Abram to understand there was more to the promise. So, he gave him a new identity by adding the Hebrew letter *hei* to his name, calling him "Abraham." The name means "father of many," which is fitting to God's promise. But there's more. The Hebrew letter *hei* is the letter of the divine breath. It represents God's creative power and potential. In the natural, there was no way that Abraham and Sarah could conceive at this point in their lives. God was reminding them that the birth would be *super*natural.

It is interesting to look at the timing of this name change in Genesis. It occurs right after the episode with Hagar, when Abraham and Sarah tried to come up with a way in the "natural" to make God's promise of a son come to pass. The Lord was telling Abraham the fulfillment of this promise would not occur in the natural. Rather, it would occur as a result of God supernaturally enabling Sarah to conceive, even though she had been barren all her life and was now advanced in years. The promise was now locked in Abraham's very name.

Sometimes, we also need a reminder about who God called has us to be and what he has promised to do in us. It's so easy to look at a situation and believe that nothing will ever change. But God reminds us that with him "all things are possible" (Matthew 19:26). We just have to believe and allow his creative power and potential to work in our lives.

Read | Genesis 17:1–19

Reflect

1. Abraham was ninety-nine years old when God appeared to him this time. God instructs him to remain faithful—to keep holding on to the promise—and again stresses

that it *will* come to pass. What does God then say about what Abraham will receive as part of the everlasting covenant that he is establishing with him?

2. When you look at where this story in placed in Genesis—the events that occurred up to this point and Abraham's advanced years—why do you think God chose this particular moment to change his name? What reminder did Abraham need at this time?

3. Think back on some times in your life when you have been in Abraham's situation. Have you ever given up on a promise from God only for him to fulfill that promise later? If so, why do you think God chose to fulfill his promise to you when he did?

4. The passage reveals that Abraham listens to God's words and then laughs at the thought of Sarah bearing a child at the age of ninety. But God reminds him that Sarah will bear him a son—and they are to call him Isaac, which means, "he laughs." In what area of your life right now do you also need a reminder that God is still actively at work?

Pray | Spend a few minutes with your heavenly Father in prayer. Ask him to remind you of his grace and his power to redeem the broken places in your life. Remember that in Christ, you also have a new name and identity: a beloved child of God (see 1 John 3:1).

—Day 4—

Called to Sacrifice

Whandding you read the account of Abraham's life, it seems that as soon as God fulfills his promise to give him and Sarah a son, the Lord asks him to give that son up as a sacrifice. However, according to Jewish tradition, Isaac was likely in his thirties at the time—which means three decades have passed between the events of Genesis 21 and 22.[15] Abraham has spent *thirty* years with Isaac, nurturing him, teaching him, watching him grow up.

Still, when are you ever ready to say goodbye to your own child? Never. Yet this is exactly what God asks Abraham to do. According to Genesis 22:4, the journey takes three days. *Three days.* That's a lot of time to consider the sacrifice of your only child.

Sacrifices were common in ancient times. Furthermore, according to once scholar, "In the ancient Near East, the god that provides fertility . . . is also entitled to demand a portion of what has been produced."[16] So, this demand would not have been unheard of for Abraham. Other tribes and cultures in the ancient Near East performed child sacrifice. It is possible that Abraham was simply thinking that God was now asking him to do the same.

We don't always understand God's ways. No one understood this better than Abraham. For him, it likely seemed that now the promised child had come, the Lord would demand that child as a sacrifice. But this is where the story takes a turn, for God had no intention of Isaac being sacrificed. Instead, he was testing Abraham's faith. As a result, this story displays human beings at their very best: trusting in the God of the How and When no matter what.

Read | Genesis 22:9–12

Reflect

1. When God calls Abraham to sacrifice his only son, there is no indication that Abraham wavered in his faith or argued with God or tried to get out of it. What does this say about Abraham and Isaac and their relationship with God?

2. Abraham never wavers in his resolve to follow God's instructions. What does God say after this ordeal that he now knows about Abraham?

3. Abraham was willing to give up the son whom he had waited more than twenty-five years for God to deliver as a sacrifice. What is something that you have sacrificed or given up recently? How did it feel to make this sacrifice—and why did you make it?

4. What is something difficult in your life right now that you sense God is asking you to do? What does this story of Abraham and Isaac reveal about God's faithfulness?

Pray | Spend a few moments in prayer. If you feel any tension with the story that you have read today, bring that to the Lord. If you are feeling called to sacrifice something in your life—your time, a habit, possessions—ask God to give you the courage to do so.

Mount Moriah. This location is first mentioned in Scripture in this passage where God instructed Abraham to sacrifice Isaac. About one thousand years after this event, King David bought a threshing floor owned by Araunah the Jebusite at this location and erected an altar there. After his death, his son Solomon built a temple on the site, which lasted for 400 years until it was destroyed by the Babylonians in 586 BC. Seventy years later, the temple was rebuilt by exiles returning from captivity. During the first century, King Herod made additions to this structure, which then became known as Herod's Temple. The structure was destroyed by Roman armies led by Titus, the son of the emperor, in AD 70. Today, all that remains is a portion of a retaining wall called the "Western Wall" or "Wailing Wall," which serves as a site of prayer for the Jewish people.[17]

-Day 5-

Leaving a Legacy

There's a reason we still talk about Abraham: *he left a great legacy*. He wasn't perfect, but he obeyed God when it mattered most. His story took time to unfold. He didn't have Isaac until he was one hundred years old. But the timing was God's and, therefore, it was perfect. Because God had a plan for Abraham, we can celebrate him and his legacy today.

The author of Hebrews would later include Abraham in a passage that we know as the Hall of Faith, in which he acknowledges the "heroes" of the faith in the Old Testament. This author defines faith in this way: "Now faith in confidence in what we hope for and assurance about what we do not see" (Hebrews 11:1). Abraham lived this definition. He hoped for things he had not seen: a son, offspring numbered by the stars, being the father of Israel. Some of these promises he lived to see. Others he didn't.

This is actually a theme among the other heroes of the faith listed in the Hall of Faith: Moses, Noah, Gideon, and Rahab, to name a few. The author of Hebrews writes, "These were all commended for their faith, yet none of them received what had been promised, since God had planned something better for us so that only together with us would they be made perfect" (verses 39–40). None of the Old Testament heroes lived to see the greatest fulfillment of God's promise of redemption through the blood of Christ.

Our faith does not always guarantee that we will see the promise fulfilled, the relationship restored, or the sick healed. But our faith does promise us the presence of God. He was with all the heroes of the faith back then . . . and he is with us still today. This is true whether our promise has come to fruition or we continue to wait for it to be fulfilled.

Read | Hebrews 11:8–10

Reflect

1. Scholars believe that Hebrews was written to a group of Jewish Christians who were being tempted to return to their former way of life before encountering the Messiah.

The author reminds them that following Christ requires risk, trust, and sacrifice—but that it is worth it. How does the author say Abraham demonstrated this faith?

2. Abraham lived "like a stranger in a foreign country" (verse 9). Although he had received the promise that his descendants would one day be a great nation, neither he nor Isaac nor Jacob experienced that reality in their lifetimes. What does the author say in verse 10 enabled Abraham to keep holding on to the God's promises?

3. Abraham left a great legacy behind because of his profound faith. Who has left a great faith legacy in your life? What do you admire most about this person's faith?

4. If someone were to write about you like the author of Hebrews wrote about Abraham in this passage, what would he or she say about your faith? What would you *want* this person to say about you, your faith, and the legacy that you will leave behind?

Pray | Spend a few minutes reflecting on this week's personal study time. Did God convict you of anything this week? Did you change in any way or learn something new? Talk to God about what you discovered in his Word this week and what he might be showing you today.

For Next Week

Before you meet again with your group next week, read chapter 2 in *The God of the Way*. Also go back and complete any of the study and reflection questions from this personal study that you weren't able to finish.

Schedule

WEEK 3

BEFORE GROUP MEETING	Read chapter 2 in *The God of the Way* Read the Welcome section (page 57)
GROUP MEETING	Discuss the Connect questions Watch the video teaching for session 3 Discuss the questions that follow as a group Do the closing exercise and pray (pages 57–68)
PERSONAL STUDY – DAY 1	Complete the daily study (pages 70–71)
PERSONAL STUDY – DAY 2	Complete the daily study (pages 72–73)
PERSONAL STUDY – DAY 3	Complete the daily study (pages 74–75)
PERSONAL STUDY – DAY 4	Complete the daily study (pages 76–77)
PERSONAL STUDY – DAY 5 (before week 4 group meeting)	Complete the daily study (pages 78–79) Read chapter 3 in *The God of the Way* Complete any unfinished personal studies

Sarah

REFLECTING GOD'S BEAUTY

When Abram came to Egypt, the Egyptians saw that Sarai was a very beautiful woman. And when Pharaoh's officials saw her, they praised her to Pharaoh, and she was taken into his palace. He treated Abram well for her sake, and Abram acquired sheep and cattle, male and female donkeys, male and female servants, and camels.

GENESIS 12:14–16

Israel in Sarah's Day

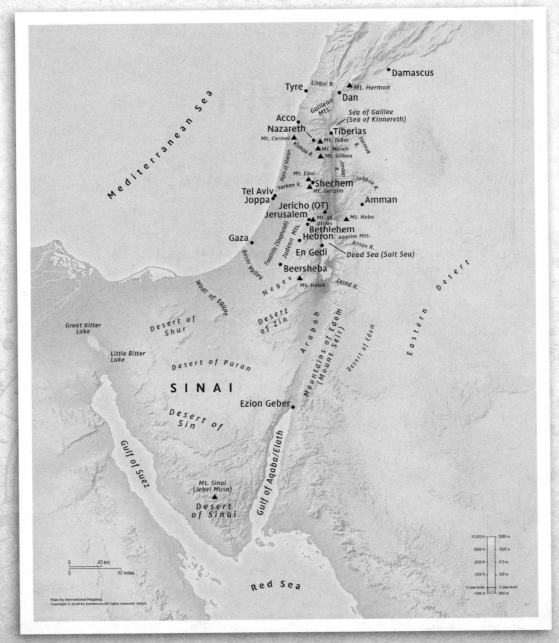

Welcome | Read On Your Own

In the last session, you looked at the story of Abraham and how God promised to give him a son in his old age and make his descendants into a great nation. Entwined with Abraham's story is the story of his wife, a woman the Bible reveals was named Sarai before God changed her name to Sarah. She trekked alongside her husband from the beginning when God called them both to leave the land of Ur of the Chaldeans and make the long journey westward toward Canaan.

It can be easy to overlook this fact, given that so much of the story of God's covenant in Genesis focuses on Abraham. Yet the Bible reveals that when God called Abraham to leave his homeland, "[Abraham] took his wife [Sarah], his nephew Lot . . . and they set out for the land of Canaan, and they arrived there" (Genesis 12:5). She, too, heard the promises of land, blessing, and an heir. She, too, trusted in God's faithfulness to guide and sustain them along the way. And she, too, struggled at times in waiting on God's timing for this promise to come to pass.

Sarah was strong, independent, resourceful . . . and *beautiful*. On two occasions, we read that Abraham was so fearful that people would see his wife's beauty and want to kill him that he lied and said she was his sister (see 12:11–13; 20:1–2). This was actually a *half*-truth, for Sarah was Abraham's *half*-sister (see 20:12). Each time, the citizens did see that Sarah was a beautiful woman, and each time she was taken into the king's palace (see 12:16; 20:2). Sarah also had great inner beauty. The name that God gave to her, Sarah, means "princess," and in Jewish thought, the true beauty of a princess is what resides within.

In this session, you will take a closer look at this remarkable woman to see how, at times, she differed from Abraham in her response to God's promise. You will look again at the story of Hagar to get a better idea of the events from Sarah's perspective and how the birth of Ishmael caused contention. You will also explore what the Bible says about beauty and why it is so critical to reflect God's beauty to the world. Finally, you will see that Abraham and Sarah's stories are not just tales from the ancient past but have practical meaning for your life today.

Connect | 15 minutes

Welcome to session 3 of *The God of the How and When*. To get things started for this week's group time, discuss one of the following questions:

- What is a key insight or takeaway from last week's personal study that you would like to share with the group?

— *or* —

- What comes to mind when you think about reflecting God's beauty to the world? What would that involve on your part?

Watch | 20 minutes

Now watch the video for this session. As you watch, use the following outline to record any thoughts or concepts that stand out to you.

I. How did Sarah respond to God's promise that she would have a son?

    A. Sarah was there when God spoke to Abraham. She was willing to leave her homeland and do everything that he was willing to do (see Genesis 12:4–5).

        1. However, when God visited the couple and said Sarah would have a child in one year's time (see Genesis 18:10), she responded differently to the promise than Abraham.

        2. The Bible says she "laughed to herself" when she heard the news (Genesis 18:12). The Hebrew word, *sachaq*, refers to laughing in a derisive, scoffing, or mocking manner.

B. God ultimately changed Sarah's heart and helped her to have faith in him.

    1. Instead of laughing *at* God's promises, she wound up laughing *with* God's promises

    2. Sarah and Abraham did have a son a year later, and they named him Isaac, or *Yitzak* in Hebrew, which means "he will laugh" or "he laughs."

C. When God gives us a promise, there are two responses we can make.

    1. *We can laugh at the promises of God.* When we do this, we are attacking the promise that God has made over our lives. We don't want to minimize God's promises to us.

    2. *We can laugh with the promises of God.* When we do this, we learn to laugh and be joyful regardless of our present situation or the circumstances we face.

What's in a Name?

Both Abram and Sarai received new names from God that reflected aspects of the covenant he was making with them. Abram became Abraham, and Sarai became Sarah. But this couple in the Bible are not the only individuals who received new names. The following represent just a few of the other notable name changings that are recorded in Scripture.

Jacob ➔ Israel. The name Jacob means "grasps the heel" or "supplanter." He was given this name by his mother, Rebekah, because he grasped the heel of his twin brother, Esau, when the two were born (see Genesis 25:26). God changed his name to Israel, "wrestles with God," after he literally wrestled all night with God at the river Jabbok (see 32:28).

Joseph ➔ Zaphenath-Paneah. The name Joseph means "God will add." He received this name from his mother, Rachel, who had previously been unable to conceive (see 30:24). When Joseph rose to power in Egypt, the Pharaoh gave him the name Zaphenath-Paneah to assimilate him into Egyptian culture, which likely means "the god speaks and he lives" (see 40:25).

Hoshea ➔ Joshua. The name Hosea means "saves" or "salvation." As we will discuss in a future session, Moses changed his name to Joshua, meaning "the Lord saves," when he was sent out to investigate the land of Canaan and report back to the people (see Numbers 13:16).

Naomi ➔ Mara. The name Naomi means "pleasant," but when she suffered a number of crises in her life, she changed her name to Mara, which means "bitter" (see Ruth 1:20).

Daniel ➔ Belteshazzar. Daniel means "God is judge," while Belteshazzar means "Bel protects his life," with Bel being the chief Babylonian deity. He received this name from Ashpenaz, a court official, to assimilate him into Babylonian society. Ashpenaz also changed the names of Daniel's friends Hananiah, Mishael, and Azariah to Shadrach, Mesach, and Abednego. Each of these names were changed as a way of encouraging the young men to forget the God of Israel and become conformed to the gods of Babylon (see Daniel 1:6–7).

Simon ➔ Peter. The name Simon means "listen" or "hearing," but Jesus changed it to Peter, meaning "rock," when the disciple professed that Christ was "the Messiah, the Son of the living God" (Matthew 16:16). Jesus prophesied that Peter would become a "rock" on which the foundation of the church would be built, which proved to be true (see Acts 2:14–41).

II. Why did God change Sarah's name?

    A. The name Sarai means "to contend" or "to be contentious." We see this character trait in her interactions with Hagar, her handmaiden.

        1. Sarah, fearing God's promise of a son will not come to pass, instructs Abraham to have a child with Hagar, and she will raise that child as if it is her own (see Genesis 16:1–2).

        2. Hagar begins to look down on Sarah when the child is born to her (see Genesis 16:4). So Sarah *contends* with Hagar over who will be the head of the house (see verses 5–6).

        3. God changes Sarai's name to Sarah by adding the Hebrew letter *hei.* The name Sarah means "princess," which shows how beloved she was in God's sight.

    B. We shouldn't be quick to judge Sarah.

        1. Waiting is difficult, and being patient with the promises of God is difficult. It's understandable why Sarah, after waiting so many years, would grow impatient.

2. We have to trust God with the *how* and with the *when*. When we try to take matters into our own hands, it never works out well for us.

III. Sarah was one of the most beautiful women—if not *the* most beautiful woman—in Scripture. What can we learn from the Bible about this concept of beauty?

   A. Sarah's beauty was a blessing, but it also caused trouble at times.

   1. When Abraham went to Egypt, he was concerned that the Egyptians would see Sarah's beauty and want to take his life. So he told her to say that she was his sister (see Genesis 12:10–13).

   2. When Abraham later went to Gerar, he again instructed her to say that she was his sister. Abimelek, the king, sent for Sarah and took her (see Genesis 20:1–2).

   3. One of the things the story of Sarah reveals is that *beauty is our birthright*. God does not do ugly. When he created the world in the beginning, he created it *beautiful*.

B. There is a connection in the Bible between Sarah and Esther.

    1. Scripture says that Sarah lived 127 years. Esther ruled over 127 provinces. The rabbis make a connection between Sarah and Esther on the basis of the number 127.

    2. In Jewish thought, the beauty of a princess is within. We see this in Esther's story. The name Esther means "I will hide." Esther's true beauty was hidden within her.

C. Sarah is considered an even greater prophet than Abraham.

    1. When Sarah told Abraham that Hagar's son, Ishmael, had to be put out, Abraham was reluctant to do it. But God told Abraham to do what Sarah was telling him to do (see Genesis 15:9–13).

    2. Based on this, the rabbis say that Sarah was a greater prophet than Abraham, because she heard God's voice more clearly.

The Most Beautiful Women in Scripture

"The Sages taught: There were four women of extraordinary beauty in the world: Sarah, and Abigail, Rahab, and Esther."[18] This statement from the Talmud, the central text of Rabbinic Judaism, identifies the woman that we've been studying in this session—Sarah—as one of the most beautiful in Scripture. But what do we know about the other three?

Rahab. We first encounter Rahab when the Israelites were preparing to conquer the city of Jericho under the leadership of Joshua. In preparation for the attack, Joshua sent two scouts to survey the city's defenses and report back, and the men were hidden by Rahab. When the king of Jericho learned there were spies in his city, he commanded Rahab to reveal them. But Rahab refused, telling the king the men had already left. As a reward for her service, she and her household were spared from the destruction of the city. The Bible states that Rahab was a prostitute but nowhere mentions her beauty (see Joshua 2:1–24; 6:17).

Abigail. This remarkable woman makes an appearance in the Bible during the time that David is on the run from King Saul. David and his army learn that a wealthy man in the region, named Nabal, is shearing sheep and asks for his support. But Nabal refuses, prompting David to issue an order for his army to forcibly take what they need. At this point, Abigail, the wife of Nabal, intervenes and pleads with David to hold off the attack. Her words and gifts convince David to stand down. When Nabal dies ten days later, David takes Abigail as his wife. She is described in Scripture as both intelligent and beautiful (see 1 Samuel 25:1–44).

Esther. We know more about Esther than the others on this list, for there is an entire book of the Bible that explains how she saved her people from destruction. Esther was a Jewish exile living in the city of Susa in Persia who became the wife of King Xerxes. One day her cousin, Mordecai, offends a Persian official named Haman by refusing to kneel when he passes by. Haman learns that Mordecai is a Jew and hatches a plot to kill all the members of his race. Ultimately, Esther decides to go before the king even though she has not been invited—an action that could lead to her death. In the end, the plot is exposed, Haman is put to death, and the Jews are allowed to bear arms to defend themselves (see Esther 1–10).

D. The Hebrew word used to describe the making of the woman is different than the word in Hebrew used to describe the making of the man.

    1. The Hebrew word for the making of the woman is *banah,* which means "to build" (see Genesis 2:22), but it is also connected to the word *binah,* which means "insight or discernment." God makes the woman in such a way that she has *binah.*

    2. A man cannot reflect the image and likeliness of God apart from the woman. It's only the two together that fully reflect the image, glory, and goodness of God.

IV. What can we learn from Sarah's story in our modern world?

    A. *Don't snicker at the promises of God.* Even when those promises seem impossible, stay true to believing that God can bring them to pass.

    B. *Remember that God's timing is not your timing.* God's timeline is different from our timeline. Often it takes a long time to come to pass, and we have to be patient in the waiting.

Discuss | 35 minutes

Take some time to discuss what you just watched by answering the following questions. There are some suggested questions below to help you begin your discussion, but feel free to pick any of the additional questions as well as time allows.

Suggested Questions

1. Sarah was a woman of faith. She left her hometown in Ur of the Chaldeans when God called and journeyed with Abraham to Canaan. She received the same promise of an heir as her husband received. Yet what was different in the way she responded when the Lord visited her years later and said she would bear a son (see Genesis 18:10–12)?

2. The name Sarai means "to contend" or "to be contentious," and we see this character trait in her interactions with Hagar, her handmaiden. When Sarah began to worry that God would not fulfill his promise of an heir, she came up with a plan for Abraham to carry on the family line by having a child with Hagar (see Genesis 16:1–2). How did this plan soon go awry and lead to contention and strife in the household?

3. Read 1 Peter 2:9. In Sarah's day, women who were barren were looked down upon by others in society and suffered a great deal of shame. However, the name that God gave to her—Sarah—means "princess." What does this say about the way in which God saw her? What does this passage in 1 Peter say about the way that God sees *you*?

4. Read James 1:2–3. Sarah's story reveals that when God gives you a promise, you can either laugh *at* that promise (and not believe it will come to pass), or you can laugh *with* that promise (and rejoice that God will make it come to pass). What does this passage in James say about being joyful even when you are faced with trials? What helps you to remember God's faithfulness when you are going through difficult times?

Additional Questions

Read Genesis 2:22. The Hebrew word used to describe the making of the woman in this verse is *banah*, which means to build, but is also connected to the Hebrew word *binah*, which means discernment. It is only the man and woman together, complementary, that reflect the full image of God. What are some of the challenges you have experienced when it comes to this type of complementary relationship between men and women?

5. Abraham is revered as a great prophet to whom God chose to reveal himself. However, the rabbis say that Sarah was an even *greater* prophet than Abraham, because she was able to hear God's voice more clearly. What are some examples of this in the Bible? What does this say about the way that God uses all kinds of people for his purposes?

6. It is easy to find fault with Sarah for moving ahead of God's timing and trying to secure an heir through Hagar. However, we have to remember that she and Abraham waited *twenty-five years* from the initial promise of a son to the fulfillment of that promise. How do you think *you* would have responded if you were asked to wait that long for something God promised to you? Why it is so hard at times to just wait?

7. Read Lamentations 3:22–26. What does it mean that God's mercies are "new every morning"? What is the promise in these verses for those who choose to "wait quietly" on the Lord—even when they don't know *how* or *when* that he will act on their behalf?

Respond | 10 minutes

Review the outline for the video teaching and any notes you took. In the space below, write down your most significant takeaway from this session.

Pray | 10 minutes

End your time by praying together as a group, asking the Lord to help you reflect his beauty to the world. Ask if anyone has any prayer requests to share. Write those requests down in the space below so you and your group members can pray about them in the week ahead.

Name	Request

Personal Study

As you discussed in your group time this week, sometimes God will ask you to trust in him even when the way forward seems impossible. Sarah certainly had her doubts when God appeared to her in her old age and reiterated his promise that she would give birth to a son. The idea seemed so preposterous and so unbelievable that she laughed out loud at God's words! Yet God proved to be faithful in her story . . . and he will prove to be faithful in yours if you trust him to provide the *how* and *when* of his promises. As you explore these themes in the life of Sarah this week, be sure to write down your responses to the questions in the spaces provided, as you will be given a few minutes to share your insights at the start of the next session. If you are reading *The God of the Way* alongside this study, first review chapter 2 in the book.

-Day 1-

The Burden of Infertility

The first thing we learn about Sarah in the Bible is related to her fertility: "Now Sarai was childless because she was not able to conceive" (Genesis 11:30). Quite an introduction! Couldn't the writer have led off with some other description of her? In truth, the fact the writer of Scripture opens with Sarah's infertility says a lot about the culture in which she lived.

Back in the time of Abraham and Sarah, if a woman was unable to have children, it greatly disrupted the ancient family system, the inheritance line, and the ability for the couple to be cared for in their old age.[19] Interestingly, infertility is a common theme that runs throughout the Old Testament. The "foundational mothers of ancient Israel," which include Sarah, Rebekah, and Rachel, were all at one time barren. When these women did conceive, it was because of God's intervention.

Sarah, Rebekah, and Rachel all bore sons who were "foundational ancestors of the nation of Israel."[20] But before their fertility was barrenness—years of yearning for the one thing that would put them in good social standing and the one thing they desired most: *a child*.

Perhaps you've experienced infertility and the rollercoaster of hope . . . disappointment . . . hope . . . and disappointment again. Perhaps you've experienced a lack of life elsewhere—in your work, your relationships, in your family. If so, know you are not alone. The foundational mothers of our faith held this pain and desire close to their hearts.

Read | Genesis 11:29–30, Genesis 25:19–21, and Genesis 29:31–30:1

Reflect

1. How is the infertility of Sarah, Rebekah, and Rachel described in these passages?

2. In the story of Rachel, we learn that she and her sister, Leah, were married to Jacob. Leah became pregnant and gave birth to four sons—Reuben, Simeon, Levi, and Judah (with two more to follow)—while Rachel remained childless. However, Leah still did not feel that she was loved by Jacob. How is this reflected in what she named her sons?

3. When Rachel saw that she was not bearing any children, she cried out to Jacob, "Give me children, or I'll die!" (Genesis 30:1). Have you ever felt the way Rachel did in this moment, whether it was about your own infertility or something else? If so, how would you fill in this blank: "Give me _____, or I'll die!"?

4. In the stories of Sarah, Rebekah, and Rachel, the Lord intervened and allowed these women to bear children. Sarah bore Isaac, Rebekah bore Esau and Jacob, and Rachel bore Joseph and Benjamin. How do the stories of these women resonate with you? How do they reveal that God cares about every aspect of our lives?

Pray | Spend a few moments in prayer. Bring your deepest desires before God, no matter how hesitant you are to voice them. Allow God's kindness and faithfulness to speak to these desires.

Infertility and Idolatry.
Excavations in Israel have uncovered clay fertility figures that were intended to help infertile women get pregnant through "sympathetic magic." Each figure was molded to look like a pregnant woman, and as the barren woman handled it, she hoped to take on the likeness of the figure. Of course, all such idolatrous practices were expressly prohibited by God.[21]

-Day 2-

Laughing at Hope

Hope is delicate. It rises when we sense something we longed for is going to come to pass—the fulfillment of a dream, realization of a goal, ending of a struggle. But just as quickly, those hopes can be dashed when the situation does not turn out how we expected. When that happens, we can fall into a pattern of becoming guarded, not daring to allow ourselves to hope again because the pain is too great when those hopes are dashed.

Sarah understood the up-and-down rollercoaster of hope. She would have been elated when God promised to make Abraham and her into a great nation. She would have been encouraged when God established the "covenant of the parts." She would have been reassured the promise was going to come to pass when God changed her name. But each time, God's words were followed with another extended period of waiting.

Sarah had now been waiting for this child for nearly twenty-five years. Twenty-five years of getting her hopes up, only to be let down. Year and after year of hoping *this would be the year,* only to be disappointed again. So it's little wonder, as you will read in today's passage, that when the Lord again appeared to Abraham and said that Sarah would have a child, she *laughed* at the idea. By this point, she knew where getting her hopes up would get her.

And we know too. We have hoped for the child to be born, the relationship to return, the sickness to go away. We have seen glimmers of possibility, only to be let down and left in the same spot—still waiting. It is tempting to put up our guard when this happens. It's easier to laugh, to stay in disbelief, than dare to believe. But when God makes us a promise, he is asking us to continue to hope in faith *until it comes to pass.* He wants us to believe that what he said will happen and to allow his perfect timing to lead the way.

Read | Genesis 18:9–15

Reflect

1. God had spoken to Abraham on several occasions, but this time he appears in the form of one of three visitors. Abraham, following the practices of his day, offers a meal and

a place for the visitors to rest. As the conversation progresses, one of the men states that Sarah will bear the long-promised son in a year. Why do you think that Sarah laughed when she heard this? What might have been going through her mind?

2. Even though Sarah was in the tent, and presumably some distance away from the visitors, the one who had made the promise heard her laugh. How did he react? What does this response say about the way that God felt about Sarah's laughter?

3. Put yourself into Sarah's place for a moment. Have you ever laughed at the possibility of a dream that you thought was now unreachable and impossible coming true in your life? If so, what was behind the laughter—shame, fear, anger, or something else?

4. The Lord said to Abraham, "Why did Sarah laugh . . . is there anything too hard for the LORD?" (verses 13–14). When you are hesitant to hope for something, what is it that you're not believing about God, who he is, or what he's capable of?

Pray | End your time in prayer. No matter where you are on the spectrum of hope—hopeful, cynical, hesitant, or somewhere in between—bring the state of your heart before the Lord. Let him give you the healing, hope, or comfort you need today.

— Day 3 —

The Promise Is Fulfilled

God did fulfill his promise to Sarah. At the age of ninety, she and Abraham welcomed their first child into the world. This time, she laughed with *joy*. She named the child Isaac, which actually means "laughter."[22] God had turned her hurt, pain, and doubt into the fulness of joy.

The story of Isaac's birth begins with these words: "Now the LORD was gracious to Sarah as he had said, and the LORD did for Sarah what he had promised" (Genesis 21:1). The Hebrew word translated as "was gracious" is a term that signifies great care and concern. It's the same word translated as "remember" in Genesis 8:1: "But God remembered Noah." And Exodus 2:24: "God . . . remembered his covenant with Abraham, with Isaac and with Jacob."[23]

God remembered Sarah, even though the promise took twenty-five years to be fulfilled, even though Sarah laughed at God's plan, and even though she tried to make her own plan. God did not remove his grace from her. He did not go back on his promise when she doubted, or when she laughed, or when she grew impatient with all the waiting. The Lord's faithfulness to Sarah did not depend on her faithfulness to him. He fulfilled his promise of a son to her simply because he had promised to do so. And he is always faithful to fulfill his promises.

This is why our stories are capable of redemption. This is why our laughter can turn from cynicism to joy. This is why we can dare to put our hope in God and believe that he will come through for us. For our God is gracious with us and always does what he says that he will do.

Read | Genesis 21:1–7

Reflect

1. The account of Isaac's birth seems almost anticlimactic at this point. Certainly, more pages in Genesis are devoted to the promise and announcement of this birth than

the actual event that takes place here. Why do you think this might be the case? According to verse 2, exactly when did Sarah become pregnant and bear a son?

2. Take a moment to review Genesis 16:1–6 and Genesis 18:9–15. What is the difference between Sarah's words and demeanor in this passage versus those passages?

3. Put yourself in Sarah's place. What gift, promise, or surprise from God has made you laugh with joy? What caused you to respond in that way?

4. After all those years of waiting—all the ups and down, starts and stops, steps and missteps—Sarah to look at those around her and say, "God has brought me laughter, and everyone who hears about this will laugh with me" (verse 6). What hope can you draw from Sarah's story as it relates to your own life? Explain.

Pray | End your time in prayer. If you are still waiting on a promise from God, ask him for the fullness of joy that Sarah experienced. If God has been gracious to you, thank him for his faithfulness.

-Day 4-

The Consequences of Impatience

Impatience, desperation, anger, confusion. Whenever we act from those emotions, it doesn't go well for us. We overreact. We lash out. We make rash decisions. We've all been there.

Sarah had been there too. As you saw in a previous study, when years had passed and she hadn't been able to conceive, she devised a plan for Abraham to start a family with Hagar, her Egyptian slave. In the culture of the day, it was lawful for a man to impregnate a slave girl if his wife had not produced an heir.[24] So Sarah was simply following a common practice of the time, finding a solution to her problem. But, of course, this was not God's plan.

Problems immediately emerged after Hagar's son was born. She began to "despise her mistress" (Genesis 16:4). Sarah, in turn, "mistreated Hagar" (verse 6), causing her run away. The Lord met Hagar in the wilderness and told her to "go back to your mistress and submit to her" (verse 9). So Hagar returned. But it's evident that things didn't improve in the family.

In fact, as you will see in today's reading, tensions in the household again rose to the surface after Isaac was born. This time it was Ishmael, the son of Hagar, mocking Isaac. When Sarah saw what was happening, she told Abraham to send the two of them away. Abraham was caught in the middle. He loved Ishmael and didn't want to send him off. But Sarah proved to be the "greater prophet," for God told Abraham to listen to her and do what she said.

In the end, Abraham and Sarah's plan not only failed to solve the problem but also created greater problems for everyone. The same will be true of any plans that we make outside of God's will. As the proverb states, "Many are the plans in a person's heart, but it is the LORD's purpose that prevails" (Proverbs 19:21). If we want to avoid the consequences of impatience, we have to learn how to faithfully wait on God's timing.

Read | Genesis 21:8–21

Reflect

1. It is easy to criticize Sarah's actions in this story, but at stake was Ishmael casting shame on the one whom God had designated to inherit the blessings promised to Abraham. How is this concern reflected in Sarah's words to Abraham in verse 10?

2. Abraham understood that the dynamics in the family needed to change, but the idea of sending Ishmael away greatly distressed him. After all, he was still Abraham's son. But what reassurance did he receive from God that this was the right choice?

3. Paul wrote, "Do not be deceived: God cannot be mocked. A man reaps what he sows" (Galatians 6:7). Think about a time you acted in desperation to get something you wanted and later regretted it. What did you do? What was the result?

4. Even though God instructed Abraham to follow Sarah's advice and send Hagar and Ishmael away, the Lord watched over them and kept them from perishing in the desert. How does this story demonstrate God's mercy even when we make mistakes?

Pray | Spend a few moments in prayer. Consider the plans you've been making lately. Are they God's plans or your plans? Speak honestly about them with the Lord.

The Seven Great Women Prophets.
The rabbis note that God himself attested to Sarah being a prophet when he told Abraham to "listen to whatever Sarah tells you" in the matter of sending Hagar and Ishmael away (Genesis 21:12). In Jewish tradition, Sarah is listed as one of the "seven great women prophets" of the Bible, with the others being Miriam, Deborah, Hannah, Huldah, Abigail, and Esther.

— Day 5 —

Sarah's Legacy

We saw in a previous study that Abraham is included in the "Hall of Faith" passage in the book of Hebrews. "By faith Abraham, when called to go to a place he would later receive as his inheritance, obeyed and went, even though he did not know where he was going" (Hebrews 11:8). But Sarah is included in that passage as well. Her legacy is strong—a woman who waited on the Lord . . . not always perfectly, but ever faithfully.

When God changed Sarah's name, it revealed that he viewed her as a "princess" or a "noblewoman." Yet we have to wonder how often Sarah felt that she was living up to this name. Did she feel like a princess when she was childless and unable to produce an heir? Did she feel noble when she resorted to the custom of producing an heir through a slave? Still, today, we consider her as we do royalty. We tell her story as we do the other great heroes in the Bible. While Sarah might have doubted at times whether she would live up to *anything* as a woman who could not have children, she is listed among the heroes of our faith.

And this is not because Sarah did end up having a child. And it's not because God fulfilled his promise to her. Sarah's legacy is that she journeyed faithfully with God. She endured hardship. She made mistakes. And she experienced God's grace. This is a legacy that we can *all* share—simply journeying with God as we experience the ups and downs. The rock bottoms and mountain tops, all the while feeling his presence and hearing his voice.

Read | Hebrews 11:11–13

Reflect

1. We have seen how Sarah experienced ups and downs as she waited for a son to be born. But according to verse 11, what did Sarah still consider God to be?

2. The author of Hebrews writes that "all these people"—which included Sarah—"were still living by faith when they died" (verse 13). This was an incredible legacy to leave behind. What else does the author say about Abraham and Sarah receiving the things that had been promised to them? What does this say about their level of faith?

3. As you look back on Sarah's story, what inspires you the most about her faith? Why?

4. Do you know anyone with the type of faith that Sarah demonstrated—a type of faith that weathers the ups and downs of life and remains devoted to God? If so, who is this person? What traits and qualities do you most respect about him or her?

Pray | Spend a few minutes reflecting on this week's personal study time. Did God convict you of anything this week? Did you change in any way or learn something new? Talk to God about what you discovered in his Word this week and what he might be showing you today.

For Next Week

Before you meet again with your group next week, read chapter 3 in *The God of the Way*. Also go back and complete any of the study and reflection questions from this personal study that you weren't able to finish.

WEEK 4

BEFORE GROUP MEETING	Read chapter 3 in *The God of the Way* Read the Welcome section (page 83)
GROUP MEETING	Discuss the Connect questions Watch the video teaching for session 4 Discuss the questions that follow as a group Do the closing exercise and pray (pages 83–94)
PERSONAL STUDY – DAY 1	Complete the daily study (pages 96–97)
PERSONAL STUDY – DAY 2	Complete the daily study (pages 99–100)
PERSONAL STUDY – DAY 3	Complete the daily study (pages 101–102)
PERSONAL STUDY – DAY 4	Complete the daily study (pages 103–104)
PERSONAL STUDY – DAY 5 (before week 5 group meeting)	Complete the daily study (pages 106–107) Read chapter 4 in *The God of the Way* Complete any unfinished personal studies

Moses

STRENGTH THROUGH STRUGGLES

"The Lord said to [Moses], 'Take off your sandals, for the place where you are standing is holy ground. I have indeed seen the oppression of my people in Egypt. . . . Now come, I will send you back to Egypt.' This is the same Moses they had rejected with the words, 'Who made you ruler and judge?' He was sent to be their ruler and deliverer by God himself, through the angel who appeared to him in the bush. He led them out of Egypt and performed wonders and signs in Egypt, at the Red Sea and for forty years in the wilderness."

ACTS 7:33–36

The Exodus

Maps by International Mapping.
Copyright © 2008 by Zondervan. All rights reserved. v0220.

Welcome | Read On Your Own

In the last session, you looked at the story of Sarah and how God turned her laughter of doubt into laughter of joy when Isaac, the promised son, was born. As she said, "God has brought me laughter, and everyone who hears about this will laugh with me" (Genesis 21:6). The Bible states that Isaac grew up and married Rebekah, who bore him a son named Jacob. In Jacob's later years, a famine in Canaan forced him to relocate his family to the land of Egypt.

The descendants of Jacob multiplied in Egypt during the centuries that followed. Eventually, a king arose in Egypt who viewed this growing people group as a threat, so he put them into slavery and declared that all Hebrew baby boys should be put to death. This was the situation when a child named Moses was born. His mother, fearing for his life, placed him in an ark made of bulrushes and laid him in the reeds by the banks of the River Nile.

Ironically, it was the king's own daughter who discovered the child. She raised him as her own, while his true mother served as his nurse. Ultimately, Moses became the greatest prophet of the Hebrew Bible and a central figure in Judaism, used by God to not only free the Israelites from slavery but also to give the Ten Commandments and the Torah to them. No other leader or prophet was as loved by and revered by the Jewish people as Moses. But along the way, Moses would have to face many challenges . . . and overcome many struggles.

In this session, you will look at Moses' rocky start as a leader and how God had to convince him that he *could* lead the people out of Egypt. You see the tests that Moses had to endure, beginning with his decision to intervene when he saw an Egyptian taskmaster beating a Hebrew slave, and how those tests led Moses to completely depend on God. You will learn about the "songs" that Moses had to sing at each forty-year transitional period in his life. You will also discover why God did not allow him to enter into the Promised Land during his lifetime . . . and yet how Moses would ultimately come to this land in the time of the Messiah.

Connect | 15 minutes

Welcome to session 4 of *The God of the How and When*. To get things started for this week's group time, discuss one of the following questions:

- What is a key insight or takeaway from last week's personal study that you would like to share with the group?

— or —

• What are some of the fears that people have when it comes to speaking in front of others or being a leader? In what ways have you had these fears?

Watch | 20 minutes

Now watch the video for this session. As you watch, use the following outline to record any thoughts or concepts that stand out to you.

I. How did God prepare Moses for the calling that he had for him?

    A. God first had to help Moses see his true identity as a leader.

        1. God appears to Moses in a burning bush and tells him to redeem the children of Israel out of Egypt. But Moses is reluctant and comes up with excuses (see Exodus 3:1–4:14).

        2. God's anger burns against Moses (see Exodus 4:14). The Lord is not upset that Moses has weaknesses but that he has a lack of faith in what God is asking him to do.

        3. It is likewise easy for us to look at all our problems and all our shortcomings and say, "God, thank you, but . . ." We have to move our big *buts*.

B. When God speaks to Moses, he tells him to take off his shoes.

    1. The word for "shoes" in Hebrew is *na-alayim*, and the word for "lock" is the same word. God is telling Moses, "Your fears and insecurities are locking you out of your promise."

    2. We likewise have to unlock those barriers, obstacles, and stumbling blocks that are keeping us from stepping into the mission that God has for our lives.

II. How did God change Moses' heart?

    A. God changed Moses' heart through testing.

        1. Moses was tested when he saw an Egyptian taskmaster beating a Hebrew slave (see Exodus 2:11). He had to decide whether he was going to intervene and risk his position in Egypt.

        2. Moses was tested when he saw two Hebrew slaves beating each another. He chose to flee when one asked if he was going to kill them like he killed the Egyptian (see Exodus 2:13–14).

Shoes As Barriers

The human foot contains thousands of nerve endings that provide sensations to every part of it. These nerve endings start back at the spine and branch out as they travel down the leg. When these nerves reach the foot, they divide into more branches and sub-branches throughout the foot and toes. Some nerves (called motor nerves) control muscle movements, while others (called somatic nerves) provide sensations.[25] The somatic nerves are especially sensitive, which you've no doubt realized if you have ever stepped on something sharp.

In biblical times, just like today, people constructed shoes to create a barrier between their feet and the ground to protect themselves from these sensations of pain. This footwear appears to be a type of sandal with a sole made of wood that was fastened around the foot with straps of leather. It appears that all classes of people in Palestine wore sandals of one form or another. In Assyria, the sandal also covered the heel and side of the foot for extra protection.

In the time of Christ, we find the customs of the day did not allow the Jewish people to wear their sandals indoors. Instead, they removed them at the door, and their feet were washed before they entered the home (see Luke 7:38). The Jewish people considered it a lowly task to carry or unloose another person's sandals. We see this when John the Baptist spoke of the coming of Christ, at which time he said, "He is the one who comes after me, the straps of whose sandals I am not worthy to untie" (John 1:27).

Washing another person's feet was also considered a lowly task—one that was reserved for the lowliest of servants in the household. It is likely for this reason that Jesus chose to do this task on the night he was betrayed. Peter's reaction to the idea of Jesus, his rabbi, washing *his* feet demonstrates how unthinkable it was for him (see John 13:8). But Jesus had a lesson in humility that he wanted them to learn: "Now that I, your Lord and Teacher, have washed your feet, you also should wash one another's feet. I have set you an example that you should do as I have done for you. Very truly I tell you, no servant is greater than his master" (verses 14–16).[26]

As we have seen in the story of Moses, removing one's sandals was also a sign of reverence and a symbolic act of removing the "barriers" that come between us and God. Today, there are all kinds of barriers that we create for all kinds of reasons. Some of these barriers are good and healthy. However, there are also unhealthy barriers we create that can lock us out of our promise and potential. These are types of barriers that God wants us to remove.

3. Moses was tested in the wilderness when God told him to redeem the children of Israel out of Egypt. He had to decide if his issue with his speech was going to hold him back.

4. Testing is meant to build trust. There is no triumph without testing.

B. Moses went back to Egypt, the place he had been rejected, at eighty years of age.

1. In Hebrew, the number eighty is written with the letter *pey*.

   a. *Pey* is the number that means "the mouth," so the Hebrew letter *pey* means "mouth" and has a numerical value of eighty.

   b. *Pey* is also the letter of the Hebrew word for Passover, the word for redemption, and the letter of breakthrough.

   c. God encouraged Moses that he would empower his *pey* and use him at eighty years old. God would give Moses the breakthrough.

C. We have to likewise be willing to use our mouth, because life and death are in the power of the tongue (see Proverbs 18:21).

III. Why was God so strict with Moses in the wilderness when he disobeyed?

A. The children of Israel were near Kadesh Barnea. They are thirsty, and there is no water. So they begin to murmur, grumble, and complain against God and against Moses (see Numbers 20:1–5).

1. Moses, in the sight of the people, disobeys God by striking the rock to bring water instead of speaking to the rock (see Numbers 20:6–11).

2. God told Moses that because he lacked faith in the sight of the people, he would die in the wilderness and not lead the people into the Promised Land (see Numbers 20:12).

B. There is a principle at work that goes back to the Garden of Eden: belief and obedience lead to *blessing*, while disbelief and disobedience lead to *dismissal* from God's promises.

1. Moses was called to model something before the people and fell short. So God was not going to allow him into the Promised Land because of that lack of faith.

2. God did allow Moses to look on the land. He gave Moses the strength to climb Mount Nebo and see the land and then sent him to be with his ancestors (see Deuteronomy 34:1–6).

3. Moses ultimately made it to the Promised Land. At the Transfiguration, he appeared with Elijah and spoke with Jesus (see Matthew 17:1–3).

IV. Moses had to learn which "song" he was going to sing.

A. Moses learned to sing two different songs during his lifetime.

1. *Moses learned the song of Egypt.* He was raised in the courts of Pharaoh, where he would have learned the songs of Egypt from his Egyptian stepmom (see Exodus 2:10).

2. *Moses learned the song of Israel.* He would have also learned the songs of Israel from his biological mother, who was also his Hebrew handmaiden (see Exodus 2:8–9).

B. Moses had to decide which song he was going to sing. He chose to sing the song of Israel.

1. *Moses sang the song of Israel at age forty.* He stepped in against the Egyptian task-master and tried to defend the Hebrew slave who was being beaten.

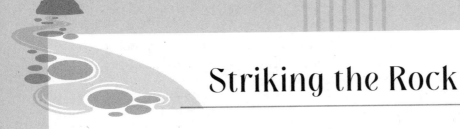

Striking the Rock

There are two stories in the Bible that tell of God providing for the Israelites in the wilderness by bringing water from a rock. The first time, the people are at Rephidim, and God instructs Moses to "strike the rock, and water will come out of it for the people to drink" (Exodus 17:6). Moses does this, the people drink, and they continue on their journey.

The second instance relates to the story that we are discussing in this session. This time, the Israelites are at Kadesh in the Desert of Zin, and God instructs Moses to "Speak to that rock before their eyes and it will pour out its water" (Numbers 20:8). But Moses disobeys and again strikes the rock. As a result, he is forbidden from entering the Promised Land.

It's a bit bewildering as to why the consequences of this one act would be so severe. After all, Moses had faithfully followed the Lord for years. But there might be more at stake here. In 1 Corinthians 10:1–5, the apostle Paul teaches that the "rock" in the desert was intended to be a picture of Christ. Here is what he writes:

> For I do not want you to be ignorant of the fact, brothers and sisters, that our ancestors were all under the cloud and that they all passed through the sea. They were all baptized into Moses in the cloud and in the sea. They all ate the same spiritual food and drank the same spiritual drink; for they drank from the spiritual rock that accompanied them, *and that rock was Christ*.

Paul says that *Jesus* was the rock following the people in the wilderness and the one from which they received the water. This is why Christ later makes this statement at the Feast of Tabernacles: "Let anyone who is thirsty come to me and drink. Whoever believes in me, as Scripture has said, rivers of living water will flow from within them" (John 7:37–38).

Some scholars believe that when God instructed Moses to strike the rock the first time, it was a picture of Jesus being sacrificed *once* to bring salvation (see Hebrews 10:12). When Moses disobeyed and struck the rock a second time, it distorted that picture—as if Jesus were being sacrificed a *second* time. Moses was to be the one that the generations that followed would look to as an example of faith, and he ultimately was to point them to the Messiah. So his unbelief and disobedience set a dangerous precedent for the people.[27]

2. *Moses sang the song of Israel at age eighty.* He accepted God's call to be the shepherd of Israel and redeem the children of Israel from Egypt.

3. *Moses sang the song of Israel at 120 years of age.* God called him home and personally buried him in Moab (see Deuteronomy 34:6).

C. In the Bible, *forty* is the number of transformative transitions.

1. Moses went through a transition every forty years. God birthed something new in him in each of these seasons that prepared him to step into a higher level of his destiny.

2. After forty years of leading the children of Israel, he experienced the greatest transition of all—entering into the presence of God in the true Promised Land in heaven.

Discuss | 35 minutes

Take some time to discuss what you just watched by answering the following questions. There are some suggested questions below to help you begin your discussion, but feel free to pick any of the additional questions as well as time allows.

Suggested Questions

1. Moses was reluctant to answer God's call when the Lord first appeared to him in the midst of a burning bush and told him to redeem the children of Israel out of Egypt. What were some of the excuses that Moses used to try and get out of the assignment? In what ways can you relate to the hesitation that Moses was expressing?

2. Moses endured several tests. He was tested when he saw the Egyptian beating a Hebrew slave. He was tested when he saw two Hebrew slaves beating each other. Now God was testing Moses by commanding him to lead the Hebrews out of Egypt. Why did God put Moses through these tests? What was God trying to teach him?

3. Read Deuteronomy 34:1–4. Moses eventually agreed to lead the people out of Egypt and faithfully walked with God his entire life. However, the Lord still prohibited him from entering into the Promised Land because of one act of disobedience, when he struck a rock to get water instead of speaking to it. Why was God so strict with Moses?

4. Read Isaiah 43:19. In the Bible, forty is the number of transformative transitions. We see this in Moses' life. Every forty years, he went through a major transition as God birthed something new in him that led to the next step of his calling. What are some of the "new things" that you sense God is doing in you in this season of your life?

Additional Questions

5. God instructed Moses to remove his shoes when he spoke from the burning bush. In Hebrew, the word for "shoes" and "lock" is the same, so God was symbolically trying to get Moses to unlock the barriers that were keeping him from accepting the mission. What are some of the ways that you have seen God unlock barriers in your life?

6. Read Romans 8:26–27. God encouraged Moses to use his words to bring freedom to the people of Israel and promised that he would give Moses the right words to say. What do these verses say about the way the Holy Spirit intercedes on our behalf when we need the "right" words to say? How has the Holy Spirit done this for you?

7. Moses had to decide what "song" he was going to sing. He could have easily chosen to continue singing the song of Egypt and not intervened when he saw the Egyptian taskmaster beating the Hebrew slave. But instead, he chose to sing the song of Israel. When is a time in your life that God has called you to "sing" a new song and step into a new role? What helped you to make that decision?

8. Read John 14:1–4. Moses ultimately experienced the greatest transition of all when he entered into God's presence in the true Promised Land in heaven. What promise does Jesus likewise make in this passage to those who faithfully follow after him? How should this promise impact the way you perceive your trials and struggles in this life?

Respond | 10 minutes

Review the outline for the video teaching and any notes you took. In the space below, write down your most significant takeaway from this session.

Pray | 10 minutes

End your time by praying together as a group, asking the Lord to shape your character through the trials you face. Ask if anyone has any prayer requests to share. Write those requests down in the space below so you and your group members can pray about them in the week ahead.

Name   Request

Personal Study

As you discussed in your group time this week, there will be times when God will ask you to step out of your comfort zone and do something for him that you don't feel qualified doing. You may question whether he has chosen the right person for the job—and even ask him to please choose someone else. However, just as Moses discovered, when you are willing to take that first uncomfortable step of faith, the Lord will be with you and guide you along the way. As you explore these themes in the life of Moses this week, be sure to write down your responses to the questions in the spaces provided, as you will be given a few minutes to share your insights at the start of the next session if you are doing this study with others. If you are reading *The God of the Way* alongside this study, first review chapter 3 in the book.

-Day 1-

Holy Ground

When God appeared to Moses in the burning bush, he said that he had heard the Israelites' cries and promised to deliver them from slavery. For Moses, this promise must have seemed like a dream too good to be true. After all, the Israelites had been in slavery for hundreds of years. Entire generations had come and gone who never knew freedom. As God's people groaned and cried out to him, they must have wondered, *Will God ever free us*?

From the outset, God revealed that he had a part for Moses to play in this plan. God was giving Moses a holy calling that could only be accomplished by a holy God. Part of this is seen in the fact that God instructed Moses, " 'Take off your sandals, for the place where you are standing is holy ground' " (Exodus 3:5). This is likely a reference to the priests who removed their sandals before entering the temple to ensure they didn't bring any dust or impurities into a holy place.[28] God's instructions reinforced to Moses that this was a holy calling.

The Hebrew word translated *holy* is *qodesh*, which means "apartness and sacredness."[29] When God calls us to do something, it's a holy work. (See "A Holy Calling" on page 98.) It's not like when our boss, spouse, or friend asks us to do something. No, when God calls us, it's different. We should expect the unexpected. We should expect miracles. We should treat that call like it is the highest in our lives, one that causes us to do what Moses did—revere God and listen to what he has to say.

Read | Exodus 3:4–10

Reflect

1. The Lord could have called out to Moses from the sky or appeared in front of him to issue his call. But instead, he took the form of a burning bush that was not consumed

and allowed this "strange sight" to compel Moses to come to him. What does God then say to him? How is the Lord's holiness described in this passage?

2. God identifies himself to Moses as "the God of your father, the God of Abraham, the God of Isaac and the God of Jacob" (verse 6). How does Moses respond when the Lord says this to him? Why do you think he reacted in this way?

3. God instructs Moses to remove his sandals, for the place where he is standing is "holy ground" (verse 5). When have you felt like you were standing on "holy ground" in the presence of the Lord? What did God's holiness feel like in that moment?

4. God revealed to Moses that he had a holy calling on his life. Do you sense that you have a holy calling on your life? If so, what is it, and how do you know it is from God?

Pray | Come before the Lord in prayer. Remember that when you pray, you are in the presence of God, standing on holy ground. Remove your shoes if that feels right and lift up your prayer with a sense of reverence and awe before the holy one who hears you.

A Holy Calling

The type of commission that God gives to Moses can be considered a "holy calling" in every sense of the phrase. The Lord was *calling* out to Moses from a burning bush. He was setting Moses *apart* to do this work—the very definition of *qodesh,* the Hebrew word we translate as *holy.* Furthermore, this mission was *holy* in the sense that we tend to understand the term, in that it would lead to the freedom of God's people and reveal the Lord's glory to the world.

The apostle Paul would later write to a man named Timothy, one of his co-workers in spreading the gospel, about the holy calling that he had received:

> Therefore do not be ashamed of the testimony of our Lord, nor of me His prisoner, but share with me in the sufferings for the gospel according to the power of God, who has saved us and *called us with a holy calling*, not according to our works, but according to His own purpose and grace which was given to us in Christ Jesus before time began, but has now been revealed by the appearing of our Savior Jesus Christ, who has abolished death and brought life and immortality to light through the gospel, to which I was appointed (2 Timothy 1:8–11 NKJV).

Paul asks his younger co-worker to remember a few things about the calling he had received. First, he was not to be *ashamed* of it. Timothy was not to avoid the stigma of being identified with a crucified criminal (Jesus) nor of being identified with a man in chains (Paul). Second, Timothy was to remember this calling would involve *suffering*. Just as Paul had endured persecution, imprisonment, beatings, and other physical and emotional harm because of his calling, so there would be a cost for Timothy. Third, he was to remember this calling had been given to him by God. The Lord had set Timothy *apart* to reveal this message.[30]

In the same way, as followers of Christ, we should never be ashamed of our calling but willing to do whatever God asks of us, regardless of how others might view us. We need to understand that our calling may come with a cost—whether that means not being included in some social circles, or being ridiculed by others because of our faith, or something even deeper. And we must remember that our holy calling comes from God. He has set us apart to do this work—so we need to be obedient to him and do it!

-Day 2-

An Insecure Prophet

Moses was one of the more unlikely prophets in the Old Testament. He had a tainted history. Before God appeared to him in the burning bush, he had killed an Egyptian and fled from Pharoah (see Exodus 2:11–15). He ended up in a place called Midian, and while he married there and had a son, he said he was a "foreigner in a foreign land" (verse 22). He didn't belong anywhere. He was ashamed of his past. How could God possibly use someone like him?

While Abraham's story opened with his immediate obedience to God, Moses' beginning is quite different. We aren't introduced to an obedient prophet but rather a hesitant one. He asks questions. He expresses his insecurities. Even when God proves his power through a series of miracles, Moses still asks if God can use him (see 4:2–10).

It's easy to shame Moses for this. How could he *not* believe? He was in the presence of the holy God! Yet we know insecurity all too well. We know self-doubt. We know fear. We have also asked God to send someone smarter, more competent, more outgoing, and less fearful than ourselves. We know the weight of the past that keeps us from moving forward. And we know the self-loathing that convinces us we aren't worthy of God's love, much less his calling.

But God doesn't buy it. He knows us better than we do. And he is ready to prove that we truly can accomplish whatever his purpose is for our lives.

Read | Exodus 3:11–14 and Exodus 4:1–13

Reflect

1. The Lord has told Moses that he has seen the misery of his people and has promised to rescue them. It is what the Israelites have been waiting to hear from God. But how

does Moses respond when God says that *he* will be the one to bring the people out of Egypt? What sort of doubts and insecurities does he express in this passage?

2. Notice how God is patient with Moses and addresses all his doubts and fears. How does the Lord reassure him in Exodus 3:12? How does he identify himself in verse 14?

3. The Lord even causes Moses' staff to turn into a snake and makes his hand become leprous so the Israelites will be convinced to follow him. But what other doubt does Moses express in Exodus 4:10 even after witnessing these miracles?

4. What insecurities do you have when it comes to your capabilities and God's ability to use you? How is God helping you to see yourself like Moses ultimately saw himself?

Pray | End your time in prayer. Bring any insecurities and self-doubts that you have before God. Ask *him* what he thinks of you. Wait and listen for his answer.

Day 3

An Unlikely Escape

The Moses we find leading the Israelites out of Egypt in Exodus 14 is a much different man than the one we first encounter at the burning bush. He has faced questions from the people. He has experienced setbacks. He has seen God's power in the ten plagues. Now, as the Israelites reach the Red Sea, he is about to witness perhaps the most well-known miracle in the Bible.

Six hundred thousand men plus women and children are escaping Egypt with Moses (see Exodus 12:37). But getting them to a place of safety will be no small feat, for Pharoah's army is trailing them with an enormous fleet of six hundred chariots (see 14:7). Now, as the Israelites reach the shore of the Red Sea, it seems as if they are doomed.

But God had led his people this way for a reason. The alternate route would have led the Israelites to cross into Philistine country, which was enemy territory. God knew the people's hearts. He said, " 'If they face war, they might change their minds and return to Egypt" (13:17). So God led the people around by this desert road toward the Red Sea.

God's way isn't always the easiest or the clearest. It won't always make the most sense to us in the moment. We may question where the Lord is leading us and how he will get us there. But if the events at the Red Sea can teach us anything, it's that God will make a way through the waters if he needs to do so, and that if we follow his leading, we will be safe in his care.

Read | Exodus 14:10–22

Reflect

1. Pharaoh had decided to release the Israelites from slavery, but after they had left Egypt, he had experienced a change of (hardened) heart. So he pursued them with

his horses and chariots to where the Israelites were camping beside the Red Sea. How did the Israelites react when they saw this army of Pharaoh approaching?

2. The people, in a panic, say to Moses, "It would have been better for us to serve the Egyptians than to die in the desert!" (verse 12). How does Moses respond to their outbursts? What does he tell the Israelites to do?

3. The Lord rescues his people by sending a wind to create a dry path in the sea for them to walk through and reach the other side. When has God made a way for something to happen in your life that you didn't think was possible? How did he make the way?

4. What is something impossible that you are facing in your today? Do you believe that God can make a way for you in that situation? Why or why not?

Pray | Spend a few moments in prayer. Thank God for how he has parted your "Red Seas" in the past. Ask him to give you a new imagination for how he might do this again with something that you are facing today. Thank him for his faithfulness in always being with you in your trials.

- Day 4 -

An Act of Disobedience

Moses' story takes a turn when the Israelites set up camp in a place called Kadesh. Like Abraham and Sarah before him, Moses is only human. Just because he was called by God to accomplish God's will doesn't mean that he was going to do it perfectly. The story you will read today proves this fact. As a result of Moses' actions, he is denied entry into the Promised Land.

Moses has done great things in God's service. He has led the Israelites out of slavery in Egypt. He has delivered the law to the people at Mount Sinai. He has stepped up and been the leader that God called him to be. But now, it appears that Moses will never see what God has promised to him. The land of Canaan. The land flowing with milk and honey. A land that has been hundreds of years in the waiting for God's promised people to arrive.

The cost of Moses' disobedience is high, just as it is for everyone who tries to go their own way. (See "The Disobedient Prophet" on page 105.) While God was faithful to provide for his people and water did flow from the rock in Kadesh, Moses' dreams dried up.

Not seeing the fruits of your labor can be devastating. Your work project is cancelled. The trip you painstakingly planned is delayed. The child you fostered and nurtured and cared for is returned to relatives. *What was it all for?* you wonder. *Did I make a difference? Will my time and effort pay off down the road?* Sometimes we get the answer to these questions. Sometimes we don't. It is just part of walking with the Lord—the tension of trusting him with our ultimate destination while our earthly destinations, goals, and dreams are less certain.

Read | Numbers 20:1–12

Reflect

1. The Israelites had a tendency to grumble and complain whenever they encountered hardships in the journey. So it's understandable why Moses' temper would have

flared up in this instance. Furthermore, we learn that Moses' sister, Miriam, had just died. What was the nature of the people's complaint in this instance?

2. What did God instruct Moses to do to bring water forth from the rock? What did Moses do instead? What do you think led to this act of disobedience to the Lord?

3. The consequences of Moses' disobedience were severe: "The LORD said to Moses and Aaron, 'Because you did not trust in me enough to honor me as holy in the sight of the Israelites, you will not bring this community into the land I give them'" (verse 12). Think about a time you distrusted or dishonored God. What was the result of your mistrust?

4. What is a goal you worked toward but never got to see come to fruition—a "Promised Land" that you weren't able to enter? What was that experience like for you?

Pray | End your time in prayer. If you are looking at a closed door to your Promised Land, bring your disappointment before the Lord. Know that he is with you even when you aren't in the place right now where you want to be.

The Disobedient Prophet

"[The priests] must be holy to their God and must not profane the name of their God. Because they present the food offerings to the LORD, the food of their God, they are to be holy" (Leviticus 21:6). As we have seen in the story of Moses at Kadesh, the Lord held his prophets, priests, and leaders to a high standard. One act of disobedience on Moses' part, for all the reasons we have discussed, led to him not being able to enter the Promised Land.

However, when it comes to prophets in the Bible disobeying God, the story of Jonah rises to the top as one of the most blatant examples. God's calling and command to his prophet were clear enough: "Go to the great city of Nineveh and preach against it, because its wickedness has come up before me" (Jonah 1:1). The city of Nineveh in that day was the capital of the Assyrian Empire. God was instructing Jonah to go to this imposing city—a place filled with idolatry and wickedness—and preach a message of repentance.

How did Jonah respond to this holy calling? "But Jonah ran away from the LORD and headed for Tarshish" (verse 2). The city of Tarshish was believed at the time to be toward the end of the earth. Jonah wanted to go as far away as he could to escape God's call. But it was a futile attempt. As the ship sailed out into the open waters, the storm clouds gathered, the seas arose, and soon the craft was floundering hopelessly on the waves.

Jonah knew he was the cause of the storm. So he instructed the sailors to throw him over the side of the boat, knowing this would calm the storm . . . and also end his life if God did not intervene. God did intervene by sending a great fish to swallow Jonah and then vomit him up on dry land three days later. And why did God choose to spare Jonah's life? "The word of the LORD came to Jonah a second time: 'Go to the great city of Nineveh and proclaim to it the message I give you'" (3:1). God had given Jonah a mission, and that mission had not been fulfilled. This time Jonah obeyed, preached God's message, and the city repented.

The story of Jonah teaches us several important truths about obedience. First, there is no place we can go to escape God's presence. Second, our disobedience to God will always lead to consequences. Third, it is always better to obey God the first time he calls us to do something. And finally, God's grace is greater than we can imagine—whether it is shown to an entire city of people or one disobedient prophet who got a second chance to get it right..

Day 5

In the Promised Land

Moses eventually does get to step into the Promised Land. Centuries after Moses' disobedience at Kadesh and his burial by God in the land of Moab, he makes an appearance in the New Testament in an event known as the Transfiguration. After Jesus predicts his own death, he takes his disciples Peter, James, and John to the top of a mountain with him. While on the mountain, they received a visit from Moses and the Old Testament prophet Elijah.

Traditionally, Moses and Elijah's presence on the mountain symbolizes the Law and the Prophets being fulfilled by Jesus.[31] Moses represents the Law, or the Ten Commandments, while Elijah represents the Prophets. Moses could not accomplish what Jesus accomplished. Moses was used by God to set the Israelites free, but only Jesus could set us all free from our sins. Moses led the people out of Egypt, but he could not lead them into the Promised Land. But Jesus can lead us all to our promised destination: an eternity with him.

Moses was a savior of the Israelite people in his day, but Jesus is the Savior of the world. When we look at Moses' story in the light of Christ, it is redeemed. Perhaps he never made it to the Promised Land, but he paved the way for *the* Savior to come who could redeem us all. In the following passage, we see Moses honored and recognized in the presence of Jesus. What he did was not for nothing. He saved his people, pointing us to our Savior, who has done the same.

Read | Matthew 17:1–13

Reflect

1. Prior to this this event, Jesus had told his disciples that he must "be killed and on the third day be raised to life" (Matthew 16:21). He had also said to them that "the

Son of Man is going to come in his Father's glory with his angels" (verse 27). How do Peter, James, and John get a glimpse of Jesus' glory in this scene?

2. Peter is obviously awestruck at the appearance of Jesus in his glory, and the presence of Moses and Elijah, and proposes they set up three shelters and spend some time together on the mountaintop. What happens right after Peter makes this statement?

3. Has Jesus ever revealed himself to you in a powerful way? If so, how did he do this?

4. Think back to the goal you identified in yesterday's study that you've worked toward but never got to see come to fruition. How does this story give you hope for that "Promised Land" that you didn't get to enter into in your life?

Pray | Spend a few minutes reflecting on this week's personal study time. Did God convict you of anything this week? Did you change in any way or learn something new? Talk to God about what you discovered in his Word this week and what he might be showing you today.

For Next Week

Before you meet again with your group next week, read chapter 4 in *The God of the Way*. Also go back and complete any of the study and reflection questions from this personal study that you weren't able to finish.

WEEK 5

BEFORE GROUP MEETING	Read chapter 4 in *The God of the Way* Read the Welcome section (page 111)
GROUP MEETING	Discuss the Connect questions Watch the video teaching for session 5 Discuss the questions that follow as a group Do the closing exercise and pray (pages 111–120)
PERSONAL STUDY – DAY 1	Complete the daily study (pages 122–123)
PERSONAL STUDY – DAY 2	Complete the daily study (pages 125–126)
PERSONAL STUDY – DAY 3	Complete the daily study (pages 127–128)
PERSONAL STUDY – DAY 4	Complete the daily study (pages 130–131)
PERSONAL STUDY – DAY 5 (before week 6 group meeting)	Complete the daily study (pages 132–133) Read chapter 5 in *The God of the Way* Complete any unfinished personal studies

Joshua

ZEAL FOR THE LORD

Joshua ordered the officers of the people: "Go through the camp and tell the people, 'Get your provisions ready. Three days from now you will cross the Jordan here to go in and take possession of the land the LORD your God is giving you for your own.'" . . . Then they answered Joshua, "Whatever you have commanded us we will do, and wherever you send us we will go. Just as we fully obeyed Moses, so we will obey you."

JOSHUA 1:10–11, 16–17

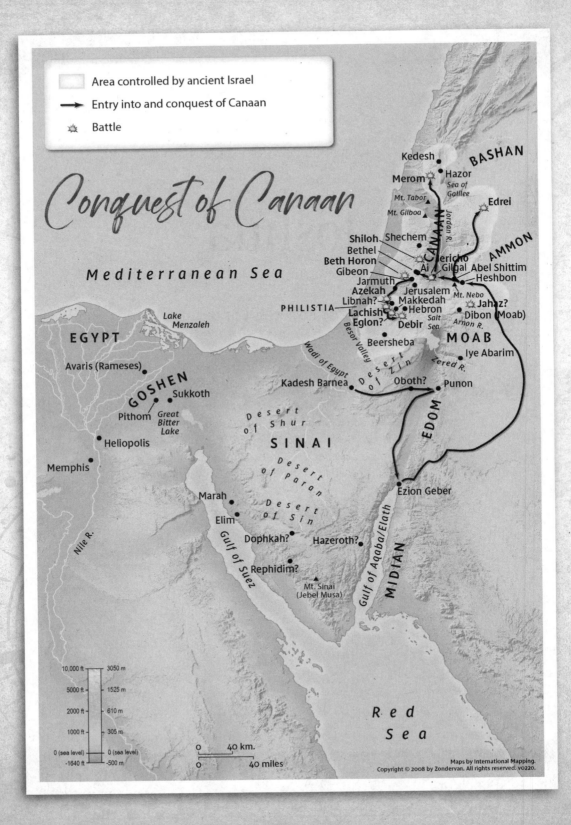

Conquest of Canaan

Legend:
- Area controlled by ancient Israel
- → Entry into and conquest of Canaan
- ✿ Battle

Mediterranean Sea

BASHAN

Kedesh
Merom ✿
Hazor
Mt. Tabor
Mt. Gilboa
Sea of Galilee
Jordan R.
Edrei ✿
AMMON
Shiloh
Shechem
Bethel
CANAAN
Beth Horon
Gibeon
Ai ✿ Jericho ✿ Gilgal
Abel Shittim
Heshbon ←
Jarmuth
Azekah
Jerusalem
Mt. Nebo
PHILISTIA
Libnah?
Makkedah
Jahaz? ✿
Lachish
Hebron
Dibon (Moab)
Eglon?
Debir
Salt Sea
Arnon R.
MOAB
Beersheba
Besor Valley
Iye Abarim
Wadi of Egypt
Desert of Zin
Zered R.
EGYPT
Avaris (Rameses)
GOSHEN
Sukkoth
Pithom
Great Bitter Lake
Kadesh Barnea
Oboth?
Punon
EDOM
Heliopolis
Desert of Shur
Memphis
SINAI
Desert of Paran
Ezion Geber
Nile R.
Marah
Desert of Sin
Elim
Dophkah?
Hazeroth?
Gulf of Aqaba/Elath
MIDIAN
Rephidim?
Gulf of Suez
Mt. Sinai (Jebel Musa)

Red Sea

Scale:
10,000 ft	3050 m
5000 ft	1525 m
2000 ft	610 m
1000 ft	305 m
0 (sea level)	0 (sea level)
-1640 ft	-500 m

0 — 40 km.
0 — 40 miles

Maps by International Mapping.
Copyright © 2008 by Zondervan. All rights reserved. v0220.

Welcome | Read On Your Own

In the last session, you looked at the story of Moses and saw how God helped him to overcome his reluctance in being the one who would bring the people out of slavery in Egypt. Although Moses was not allowed to enter into Canaan because of his disobedience, God allowed him to see the land and buried him in the land of Moab (see Deuteronomy 34:6).

Moses' death meant the people were now without a leader. Fortunately, God had already named Joshua as his successor. Of course, following in Moses' sandals was not an easy task, for "no prophet [had] risen in Israel like Moses" (verse 10), and no one could ever hope to rise to his level. But even though Joshua could not equal Moses in spiritual stature, he was equal to Moses in his *zeal* to serve the Lord. He would need that zeal in the campaign the Israelites would wage to take back the Promised Land.

We first encounter Joshua when the Israelites are attacked by the Amalekites (see Exodus 17:8–16). He was with Moses at least part of the way when God called him to climb Mount Sinai to receive the Ten Commandments (see 24:13–14). Joshua was also among the twelve spies sent to investigate the land of Canaan—and one of only two who come back with a favorable report (see Numbers 13:1–14:9). Joshua then had to wander with the Israelites in the desert for forty years, but God did allow him to enter the Promised Land (see 14:30).

In this session, you will see what set Joshua apart from the other leaders whom God could have chosen to take Moses' place. You will look at the types of zeal that Joshua demonstrated and how his life and character point to that of Christ. You will also examine what the Bible has to say and doesn't have to say about his personal life. Finally, you will get a glimpse of how Joshua maintained his zeal to the very end . . . and how we can do the same.

Connect | 15 minutes

Welcome to session 5 of *The God of the How and When*. To get things started for this week's group time, discuss one of the following questions:

- What is a key insight or takeaway from last week's personal study that you would like to share with the group?

  — *or* —

- What comes to mind when you think of *zeal*? What are traits of a person with zeal?

Watch | 20 minutes

Now watch the video for this session. As you watch, use the following outline to record any thoughts or concepts that stand out to you.

I. What set Joshua apart from the other elders and leaders of Israel?

    A. Moses, before his death, prays that God will raise up a leader in his place so that the people will not be like sheep without a shepherd (see Numbers 27:16–17).

        1. According to Jewish tradition, Moses wanted one of his sons to take his place, but God wanted to raise up Joshua (see Numbers 27:18).

        2. Joshua could never be a leader at the level of Moses. God spoke to Moses face to face. He was the one who did miracles, signs, and wonders in the sight of the people.

    B. What set Joshua apart from the other elders and leaders was his *zeal*.

        1. The Bible reveals that Joshua was zealous for two things.

            a. *Joshua was zealous for the Lord.* We read that when Moses left the tabernacle, Joshua remained behind. He wanted to stay in God's presence (see Exodus 33:11).

            b. *Joshua was zealous to serve Moses.* He served Moses even from a very young age and was dedicated and passionate about doing it.

2. This kind of zeal is important in our lives.

    a. A definition of *zeal* is "energetic, enthusiastic, proactive service done unto the Lord and in fulfillment of His commandments."

    b. When we pray from a place of rote or from a place of a habit or ritual, and there's no passion or heart connection in our words, it's not going to have an impact.

II. How does the life of Joshua point toward the life of Jesus?

  A. Joshua is a "type" of Jesus—he behaves in a way that corresponds with Jesus' character.

    1. When Jesus' parents couldn't find him as a child, he ended up being in the Temple (see Luke 2:41–52). He didn't want to leave the presence of God, the house of his Father.

    2. Jesus' first public act of ministry in Jerusalem was to overturn the moneychangers' tables in the Temple courts (see John 2:13–17).

    3. Jesus lived from a place of zeal. He was the *greater* than Joshua.

    4. All of us need to have that same kind of zeal in serving, because it is zeal that helps us overcome our lethargy and our apathy.

Sheep Without a Shepherd

"May the LORD, the God who gives breath to all living things, appoint someone over this community to go out and come in before them, one who will lead them out and bring them in, so the LORD's people will not be like sheep without a shepherd" (Numbers 27:16–17).

This metaphor of God's people being like "sheep without a shepherd" appears throughout the Bible. In 1 Kings 22:17, the prophet Micaiah predicted the outcome of a battle to King Ahab, saying, "I saw all Israel scattered on the hills like sheep without a shepherd" (1 Kings 22:17). Ezekiel later prophesied against the leaders of Israel, saying the Lord would hold them accountable "because [his] flock lacks a shepherd" (Ezekiel 34:8). In the New Testament, we read that Jesus had compassion on the crowds who came to see him, "because they were harassed and helpless, like sheep without a shepherd" (Matthew 9:36).

This concept of people being like sheep without a shepherd is not a flattering one. In biblical times, just like today, sheep were not considered to be the brightest of animals. They got spooked at the smallest of things and tended to wander off into danger. What's more, because sheep have a natural herding mentality, if one wandered into harm's way (like off the side of a cliff), others were likely to blindly follow. Sheep also had trouble finding suitable pasture land and water on their own and were easy prey for predators in the region.[32]

For all these reasons (and more), the survival of sheep *depended* on a good shepherd. The shepherd would carry a *rod* (a simple stick with a knob at the end) for use against any animal that attempted to attack one of his sheep. He also carried a long *staff* (with a crook on one end) that he would use to hook and maneuver the sheep to go where he wanted them to go. For further protection, shepherds might even carry a *sling* (comprised of a leather pouch on a string) to skillfully hurl projectiles from a distance and scare off predators.[33]

These attributes of a good shepherd—and the absolute necessity for the sheep to follow his guidance and direction—are found in one of the most famous passages in all of Scripture: *"The **LORD** is my shepherd, I lack nothing. He makes me lie down in green pastures, he leads me beside quiet waters, he refreshes my soul. He guides me along the right paths for his name's sake. Even though I walk through the darkest valley, I will fear no evil, for you are with me; your rod and your staff, they comfort me"* (Psalm 23:1–4).

III. How can we worship and have the power and passion that Joshua had?

    A. *Be passionate for God's Word.* It's not enough to open a book and read a page for a devotional. Joshua wasn't reading a few verses and saying, "I've had my devotions for the day." No, he was zealous, passionate, digging in to the text. He wanted to know what it meant.

    B. *Be passionate about being a disciple of Jesus.* The word for *disciple* in Greek and Hebrew means "learner," because you can't be a lover of God if you're not a learner of his Word.

    C. *Be passionate about wielding the Word.* Everything has a spiritual dimension to it. If Jesus needed the Word of God (see Matthew 4:1–11), and Joshua needed the Word of God (see Joshua 1:7–8), how much more do we need the Word of God?

IV. What details do we know about Joshua's personal life?

    A. We know that Joshua wasn't his given name at birth.

        1. His name was Hoshea, which means "saves" or "salvation."

        2. God changes his name by adding one letter to it. The letter that God adds is the Hebrew letter *yud*. The letter *yud* represents the hand of God.

        3. Joshua needed God's hand in his life to be able to succeed. But he especially needed God's hand when the twelve spies were sent to investigate the land of Canaan.

4. The letter *yud* in Hebrew has a numerical value of ten. Joshua needed the strength of God—the hand of God—to resist the temptation to buy into the lies and the pressure of the other spies when they came back with a negative report (see Numbers 13:26–33).

B. We don't know if Joshua ever had a family.

1. In the genealogy of Ephraim given in the book of Chronicles, there is no descendant of Joshua listed, and the line ends with him (see 1 Chronicles 7:20, 26–27).

2. The Scripture's silence when it comes to Joshua's personal life is important. It tells us that Joshua, like Moses, was a sacrificial servant leader, and that was his priority.

C. Joshua remained zealous for God even into old age.

1. Joshua died at the age of 110—he lived ten years less than Moses.

2. When Joshua and Caleb were in the Promised Land, they asked for the toughest assignments, to go in and face the giants and take the land (see Joshua 14:10–11).

3. Our zeal and passion to do great things for God shouldn't diminish with old age. In fact, being older is sometimes the greatest plus for being used by God.

Typology in Scripture

In this session, we noted that Joshua is a *type* of Jesus. A *type* in Scripture can be defined as a person, place, or thing in the Old Testament that represents a person, place, or thing in the New Testament.[34] In the case of Joshua, we saw that his desire to remain in the tabernacle is a type or symbol of Jesus' desire to remain in the temple (see Exodus 33:11; Luke 2:49). This picture of Joshua in the Old Testament gives us a picture of Jesus in the New Testament.

The authors of the New Testament employed several different Greek words to communicate this idea of *type* to their readers. The first of these terms is *tupos*, from which we derive our English word *type*. This term is used in various places in the New Testament, but one notable example is Romans 5:14, where Paul writes, "Nevertheless death reigned from Adam to Moses, even over those who had not sinned according to the likeness of the transgression of Adam, who is a type [*tupos*] of Him who was to come" (NKJV).

A second term is the Greek word *skia*, which can be rendered as "shadow." In Colossians 2:16–17, Paul used this term to describe how the system of the law in the Old Testament was merely a shadow of the greater system of grace to come under Christ: "Therefore do not let anyone judge you by what you eat or drink, or with regard to a religious festival, a New Moon celebration or a Sabbath day. These are a shadow [*skia*] of the things that were to come; the reality, however, is found in Christ."

A third term is the Greek word *hupodeigma*, which can be translated as "copy." In Hebrews 8:5, the author used this term to describe how the Old Testament priestly system was a copy of what is in heaven: "[The priests] serve at a sanctuary that is a copy [*hupodeigma*] and shadow of what is in heaven." The author goes on to state, "But in fact the ministry Jesus has received is as superior to theirs as the covenant of which he is mediator is superior to the old one, since the new covenant is established on better promises" (verse 6).

A fourth term is the Greek word *parabole*, from which we get our English word *parable*. In Hebrews 9:9, the author used this term to show how the high priest entering the Most Holy Place on the Day of Atonement was an illustration of what was to come: "This is an illustration [*parabole*] for the present time, indicating that the gifts and sacrifices being offered were not able to clear the conscience of the worshiper." The author goes on to write, "But when Christ came as high priest of the good things that are now already here, he went through the greater and more perfect tabernacle that is not made with human hands" (verse 11).[35]

Discuss | 35 minutes

Take some time to discuss what you just watched by answering the following questions. There are some suggested questions below to help you begin your discussion, but feel free to pick any of the additional questions as well as time allows.

Suggested Questions

1. What set Joshua apart from the other elders and leaders of Israel was his *zeal*. When Moses left the tent of meeting and returned to the camp, "his young aide Joshua son of Nun did not leave the tent" (Exodus 33:11). What does this say about Joshua's zeal for the Lord? What does it mean in your life to have zeal for the Lord?

2. When God commanded Moses to go up Mount Sinai to receive the law, he did not go alone but "set out with Joshua his aide" (Exodus 24:13). Later, when Moses needed to send twelve men to spy out the land of Canaan, we find that Joshua was included among their number (see Numbers 13:8). What does this say about Joshua's zeal in service to Moses? Why is it critical for us to be zealous in our service?

3. Read Numbers 14:6–9. We first learn that God changed Joshua's name when he was sent to investigate the land of Canaan. The Lord changes his name from Hoshea to Joshua by adding the Hebrew letter *yud*, which represents the divine hand of God. How did Joshua need God's hand in his life when he heard the other spies' report? What report did he and Caleb give to the people of Israel and urge them to do?

4. Read Hebrews 4:12–13. When God raised up Joshua to lead the people after the death of Moses, the Lord told him to keep the Book of the Law "always on [his] lips" and

to "meditate on it day and night" (Joshua 1:8). Why do you think God gave this command to Joshua? What does the author of Hebrews say is the power of God's Word?

Additional Questions

5. Joshua could never hope to be a leader at the same level as Moses. As the Bible states, "No prophet has risen in all Israel like Moses, whom the LORD knew face to face" (Deuteronomy 34:10). How do you think Joshua felt when God called him to replace Moses? What enabled him to answer God's call and lead the people?

6. Read Matthew 6:5–8. The fact that Joshua would linger behind in the tent of meeting indicates that he had strong desire to be in God's presence and that his heart was in his prayers. What does Jesus say should likewise be our motives when coming to God in prayer? What is the warning for those who do not have their heart in their prayers?

7. The Bible is relatively silent when it comes to Joshua's personal life. We do not know if he ever married or had a family. However, the Bible is filled with stories of how he faithfully followed the Lord and led the people into the Promised Land. What does this tell us about Joshua's priorities? Why type of legacy did he leave for his people?

8. Read Psalm 71:17–18. Joshua maintained his zeal for the Lord. Even in old age, he and Caleb asked for the toughest assignments in the Promised Land. What is the psalmist's prayer in these verses that God will do for him in his old age? What are some ways you want God to use you in the next ten, twenty, or thirty years?

Respond | 10 minutes

Review the outline for the video teaching and any notes you took. In the space below, write down your most significant takeaway from this session.

Pray | 10 minutes

End your time by praying together as a group, asking the Lord to give you and your members more zeal for him. Ask if anyone has any requests to share. Write those requests down in the space below so you and your group members can pray about them in the week ahead.

Name   Request

Personal Study

As you discussed in your group time this week, when God called Joshua to lead the Israelites, he had some very big shoes to fill. There was no way that he could ever match Moses as a leader, and he could have complained to God about the unfairness of the assignment. But instead, Joshua's zeal for the Lord led him to trust that God would use the unique skills and abilities that he possessed—just as God will use the unique gifts that you possess when you choose to trust in him. As you explore these themes in the life of Joshua this week, be sure to write down your responses to the questions in the spaces provided, as you will be given a few minutes to share your insights at the start of the next session if you are doing this study with others. If you are reading *The God of the Way* alongside this study, first review chapter 4 in the book.

-Day 1-

The Spirit of Leadership

As we have seen, God would not allow Moses to enter into the Promised Land. This meant Moses needed a successor who *could* lead the people into the land to fulfill God's promise. While Moses might have had his own ideas about who that successor would be, the Lord already had just the right person in mind. God said to Moses, "Take Joshua son of Nun, a man in whom is the spirit of leadership, and lay your hand on him. . . . Give him some of your authority so the whole Israelite community will obey him" (Numbers 27:18, 20).

Joshua had been chosen as one of twelve scouts to enter Canaan ahead of the Israelites (see Numbers 13:8). Other than this, we don't know much about Joshua when he is appointed by God. However, what we soon learn is that Joshua had a great spirit of leadership that would mark his journey. He would prove to be a *great* leader who not only led the people into the Promised Land but also defeated the tribes and nations that threatened them there.

The Bible doesn't give us any indication that Joshua hesitated when God called him to a position of leadership. Unlike Moses, we don't have any stories of him arguing or bartering with God to try and get out of the assignment. This is true even though he knew that he would be attempting to fill the shoes of the greatest leader the Israelites had ever known.

Joshua was surely aware of the gravity of his position. Being called to lead isn't always comfortable, and often God calls us when we don't feel that we are ready. But following God's calling doesn't mean we have to have it all together. It simply means we are surrendered to his will. This willing heart is what allows God to work through us, teaching us to rely on his strength rather than our own so that, like Joshua, we can be strong and courageous.

Read | Joshua 1:1–6

Reflect

1. The book of Joshua opens with the announcement that Moses, the great leader and servant of the Lord, is dead. Now, it is truly time for the next generation of Israelites to rise up and take the land. What instructions did God give Joshua in this regard?

2. The Lord had previously promised to give the land of Canaan to Abraham and his descendants. What promise does God make to Joshua in this regard? What else does God promise to Joshua as it relates to his presence?

3. What leadership roles do you have at work, in your home, or in your community?

4. What hesitations did you have about stepping into those areas of leadership—whether this was a role as a parent, as a teacher, as a business manager, or as something else? How have you since grown as a leader in this role?

Pray | End your time in prayer. If you feel God calling you to lead, but you are hesitant to do so, bring your concerns to the Lord. If you've been through a season of growth in your leadership, praise God for that blessing in your life. Thank him for making you strong and courageous.

Instructing the Young

"These words which I command you today shall be in your heart. You shall teach them diligently to your children, and shall talk of them when you sit in your house, when you walk by the way, when you lie down, and when you rise up" (Deuteronomy 6:6–7).

The Israelites provided both a religious education for their children (as instructed by God in this passage) and training in practical skills that they would one day need in the workplace. In ancient Israel, it appears there were no formal schools. Most learning took place in the midst of the people's everyday lives, with the parents taking the opportunity to instruct their children as the opportunities arose throughout the day.

The religious education of children was the responsibility of the parents (see Deuteronomy 11:19; 32:46). No exceptions were made if parents thought they were too busy to teach. When the children grew up and got married, the parents still had a responsibility in playing a part in the education of their grandchildren (see Deuteronomy 4:9). Often, the families would live together and share a common home.

At an early age, children learned about the history of Israel. Often, the children would memorize a statement or creed that recounted the Israelites' history in simplified form and recite it once a year at the offering of the first fruits (see Leviticus 23:9–14). The children would learn that the nation of Israel had entered into a covenant with God, that this covenant placed certain restrictions on them, and that they had a responsibility to obey the Lord.

By the time of Christ, the Jewish people had adopted a more formal approach to education, with classrooms and teachers. Only the boys received formal training outside the home in synagogue schools, which were likely established during the exile in Babylon. In these schools, boys were required to master several key passages of Scripture, including Deuteronomy 6:4–5 (the *Shema*), Deuteronomy 11:13–21, Numbers 15:37–41, Psalms 113–119 (the *Hallel*), the Creation story in Genesis 1–5, and the sacrificial laws in Leviticus 1–8.

These schools in New Testament times were year-round. Class hours were before 10:00 AM and after 3:00 PM, with a five-hour break for the hottest part of the day. Most classrooms contained a raised platform where the teacher sat, and before him on a low rack were scrolls containing Old Testament passages. Classes were not graded by age, nor were there textbooks, so the boys sat on the ground and learned at the teacher's feet (see Acts 22:3).[36]

— Day 2 —

Day and Night

Joshua was known for being a student of God's Word.[37] For Joshua, this meant studying the Torah, or the first five books of the Old Testament. (See "Instructing the Young" on page 124.) He knew the stories of his forefathers. He knew the love and faithfulness of God and how he had directed Abraham, Sarah, Jacob, Joseph, Moses, and others to fulfill his will for their lives.

This must have been crucial for someone with Joshua's role—to lead the Israelites into the Promised Land, a land already occupied by groups who certainly didn't want the Israelites there. If a leader is going to lead, he must first be led. Joshua was led by God's Word.

Today, we not only have the Torah but also the Gospels, the epistles, the psalms, and the rest of Scripture to turn to for help, comfort, and answers. All leaders need help from time to time. They experience burnout, fatigue, and confusion. They often have to go first, carving a path for others, or they have to make big decisions that feel overwhelming. The Word of God will provide that direction. It a lamp to our feet and light to our path (see Psalm 119:105).

Even Jesus found it necessary to meditate on God's Word. He masterfully quoted Deuteronomy and other passages of Scripture when Satan tried to tempt him in the desert. He knew God's Word, but he also *was* the Word—the embodiment of God's instruction, faithfulness, and goodness. When we meditate on him and dwell in his presence, we find what Joshua likely found each time he studied the Torah: hope, comfort, and love.

Read | Joshua 1:7–9 and John 1:1–5

Reflect

1. God has just promised that he will be with Joshua and that the Israelites will take the land of Canaan. The Lord now instructs Joshua to be strong and courageous as

he prepares to lead the people into battle. What does God tell Joshua to do with the "Book of the Law"?

2. John opens his Gospel by stating, "In the beginning was the Word, and the Word was with God, and the Word was God" (John 1:1). How does John go on to describe the Word? What does the Word bring into this world?

3. The apostle Paul wrote, "Do your best to present yourself to God as one approved, a worker who does not need to be ashamed and who correctly handles the word of truth" (2 Timothy 2:15). What does it mean to correctly handle the word of truth? How would you describe what your relationship with Scripture is like?

4. God told Joshua that the "Book of the Law shall not depart from your mouth" (Joshua 1:8). What would it look like in your life if God's Word did not depart from your mouth? What is the value of meditating on Scripture and knowing in your heart what it says?

Pray | Use this prayer time to simply linger in Jesus' presence. You don't have to say anything—you can simply sit with him in silence. Practice meditating on Christ and his love for you.

—Day 3—

Stones of Remembrance

It was now time for the Israelites to enter into the Promised Land. The first place that they would attack would be the fortified city of Jericho. But standing in their way was the Jordan River, which was at flood stage at the time. The moment the Israelites crossed this river, they would be in the Promised Land. Crossing the Jordan would be a significant moment for God's people.

Joshua, following the Lord's instructions, sent priests ahead who held the ark of the covenant. "As soon as the priests who carried the ark reached the Jordan and their feet touched the water's edge, the water from upstream stopped flowing. It piled up in a heap a great distance away. The priests who carried the ark of the covenant of the LORD stopped in the middle of the Jordan and stood on dry ground, while all Israel passed by until the whole nation had completed the crossing on dry ground" (Joshua 3:15–17).

The last mile to the Promised Land would be marked with a miracle. Joshua still had a long road ahead. Many battles to be fought and wars to be won. But the people had taken the first step. So Joshua paused and marked this moment so the people would remember it.

We move through life quickly. It's easy to overlook the importance of marking our milestones and important moments. But when we take the time to do what Joshua did—when we pause to remember God, his goodness, and his faithfulness—we not only show gratitude to the Lord for what he has done but we also remind ourselves that he will always be with us. Setting "stones of remembrance" helps us remember what God did for us once and will do again.

Read | Joshua 4:1–13

Reflect

1. The Israelites followed God's instructions, and all the people crossed safely over the Jordan on dry land. In many ways, the miracle resembled the Israelites' crossing of

the Red Sea at the start of their journey when Moses led them out of Egypt. How did God then instruct the Israelites to commemorate the crossing of the Jordan?

2. Joshua called together the twelve elders of the tribe and instructed, "Each of you is to take up a stone on his shoulder, according to the number of the tribes of the Israelites, to serve as a sign among you" (verses 5–6). What was the purpose of this memorial?

3. When you look back on your life, what are some "stones" or moments in your life that represent God's faithfulness? How did the Lord act for you in those situations?

4. Which of these moments do you need to return to today? What are some practical ways that you could make it a habit to pause at times and reflect on God's goodness?

Pray | For your prayer time today, reflect on your own stones of remembrance. If it helps, write them down. Thank God for his past faithfulness and remember that he is faithful to you still.

Conquest of the Promised Land

The events in the book of Joshua can be broken into two main parts: (1) the conquest of Canaan (see Joshua 1–12), and (2) the occupation of the land (see Joshua 13–24). The conquest phase was likely completed in seven years, and the settlement phase likely took seven years as well. Here are the main highlights from these two phases:

Conquest Phase	Passage
The mobilization of the people	Joshua 1
Spies are sent to investigate the land	Joshua 2
The Israelites cross the Jordan River	Joshua 3–4
Central campaign: destruction of Jericho	Joshua 5–6
Central campaign: defeat at Ai	Joshua 7
Central campaign: conquest of Ai	Joshua 8
Treaty with the Gibeonites	Joshua 9
Southern campaign: conquest of the Amorites	Joshua 10
Northern campaign: defeat of all kings of the north	Joshua 11

Occupation Phase	Passage
Division of the land east of the Jordan to the tribes	Joshua 13
Division of the land west of the Jordan to the tribes	Joshua 14
Consignment of land to the twelve tribes	Joshua 15–19
Establishment of the cities of refuge	Joshua 20
Establishment of the cities for the Levites	Joshua 21
Reubenites, Gadites, and half of the Manasseh tribes return home	Joshua 22
Joshua's farewell address	Joshua 23
Covenant at Shechem and Joshua's death	Joshua 24

After the death of Joshua, the Israelites attempt to root out any Canaanite groups still inhabiting the land (see Judges 1:1–26). However, this effort is not completely successful (see 1:27–26) and the Israelites ultimately fall under the influence of these nations' idolatry (see 2:11–15). The Israelites existed as a loosely connected group of twelve tribes until the time of the prophet Samuel, when the leaders of these tribes asked for a king (see 1 Samuel 8–9).

-Day 4-

The Heart of a Servant

If any leader had reason to boast, it was Joshua. After crossing over the Jordan River and entering into the Promised Land, the Israelites defeated thirty-one kings and territories to the west of the Jordan over the course of seven years. (See "Conquest of the Promised Land" on page 129.) Following this, Joshua oversaw dividing this conquered land among the twelve tribes of Israel for the next seven years.[38] He was a great warrior and leader. Yet Joshua maintained the heart of a servant who never forgot the God he served.

In the New Testament, we see that Jesus led in a similar way. He said to his disciples, "The Son of Man did not come to be served, but to serve." He was the ultimate servant, eventually giving "his life as a ransom for many" (Matthew 20:28). In a realm where kings were revered for their power, Jesus flipped the dynamic upside-down. He didn't want to be a king surrounded by servants. He wanted to serve. He didn't want his followers chanting, "Long live Jesus!" He wanted to die for us.

Unlike Joshua, Jesus didn't conquer kings or territories. He spent his time talking to the marginalized and those deemed less important in society. He didn't want to be seen with rulers and powerful people. He wanted to share meals with those who were just the opposite. We still live in a realm obsessed with power and acquiring territory and wealth. But we still live in a realm Jesus claimed as his own for his own. Whenever we get caught up in the race to get to the top, we need remember that Jesus spent his time with those at the bottom.

Read | Joshua 23:1–11 and Philippians 2:5–11

Reflect

1. Joshua delivers a speech to the people "after a long time had passed and the LORD had given Israel rest from all their enemies" (Joshua 23:1). This speech would serve

as a form of farewell address. What did Joshua want the people to remember about what had happened since they entered the Promised Land?

2. Joshua had accomplished all these conquests with the help of the Lord. Yet here, his focus is on serving the people by reminding them to stay true to God. What does Joshua say about keeping the Lord's commands? Why was it important for him to stress they were not to associate with the nations that remained among them?

3. Paul asks his readers to have this same mindset of a servant in all their dealings with one another. What does he say about the humility and service that Jesus demonstrated? What is the reward for those who humble themselves and take the lowest place?

4. What do you struggle with more: serving others or leading others? Why?

Pray | End your time by reflecting on the nature of Christ in Philippians 2:5-11 or by bringing your requests to God. Ask him to show you how you can serve in your community.

– Day 5 –

The Promise Fulfilled

It was under Joshua's leadership that God's promise to Israel was fulfilled. The promise dated back to Abraham: "I will make you into a great nation" (Genesis 12:2). It continued with Moses: "I have come down . . . to bring them up out of that land into a good and spacious land" (Exodus 3:8). It concluded with Joshua: "I will give you every place where you set your foot, as I promised Moses. Your territory will extend from the desert to Lebanon, and from the great river, the Euphrates—all the Hittite country—to the Mediterranean Sea in the west. No one will be able to stand against you all the days of your life" (Joshua 1:3–5).

Abraham didn't get to see Israel grow into a mighty nation. Moses never got to step foot into the Promised Land. But Joshua got to see it all. The path to the promise had not been easy, and there had been missteps along the way—like the defeat at Ai, due to Aachan's sin, and falling for the Gibeonites' deception, due to Joshua not inquiring of the Lord (see Joshua 7–9). But in the end, Joshua led the Israelites into battle until the Promised Land was theirs.

Yes, there were areas of resistance that remained. After Joshua's death, we learn about the groups the Israelites were *not* able to drive out (see Judges 1:27–36). But they were no longer slaves of Egypt, and they were in the land of promise. Joshua got to see God's promises fulfilled. We don't always have this luxury . . . but sometimes we do. We see our prayers answered, our relationships restored, and God do what we thought was impossible.

The psalmist wrote, "Come and see what God has done, his awesome deeds for mankind!" (Psalm 66:5). When we witness the undeniable goodness of God, it is something we shouldn't forget. Instead, like the psalmist, we should praise him for his faithfulness.

Read | Joshua 21:43–45

Reflect

1. This passage in Joshua states that God gave the Israelites all the land that he had promised to their ancestors. As you look back on your own story, what is some of the

"land" that God has given to you? What are some of the victories that you can recount the Lord giving to you?

2. God also gave the people rest on every side, just as he had sworn to their ancestors. What would it look like to have rest on every side in your life?

3. Not one of the Israelites' enemies withstood them, for the Lord gave them into their hands. What is an "enemy" or struggle that you still need to overcome?

4. Not one of the Lord's good promises failed. What reassurance do you need from God today that none of his good promises to you will ever fail?

Pray | Spend a few minutes reflecting on this week's personal study time. Did God convict you of anything this week? Did you change in any way or learn something new? Talk to God about what you discovered in his Word this week and what he might be showing you today.

For Next Week

Before you meet again with your group next week, read chapter 5 in *The God of the Way*. Also go back and complete any of the study and reflection questions from this personal study that you weren't able to finish.

Schedule

WEEK 6

BEFORE GROUP MEETING	Read chapter 5 in *The God of the Way* Read the Welcome section (page 137)
GROUP MEETING	Discuss the Connect questions Watch the video teaching for session 6 Discuss the questions that follow as a group Do the closing exercise and pray (pages 137–148)
PERSONAL STUDY – DAY 1	Complete the daily study (pages 150–151)
PERSONAL STUDY – DAY 2	Complete the daily study (pages 152–153)
PERSONAL STUDY – DAY 3	Complete the daily study (pages 154–155)
PERSONAL STUDY – DAY 4	Complete the daily study (pages 156–157)
PERSONAL STUDY – DAY 5 Personal wrap-up	Complete the daily study (pages 158–159) Connect with your group about the next study that you want to go through together

Mary

RESPONDING IN HUMILITY

Mary was pledged to be married to Joseph, but before they came together, she was found to be pregnant through the Holy Spirit. Because Joseph her husband was faithful to the law, and yet did not want to expose her to public disgrace, he had in mind to divorce her quietly. But after he had considered this, an angel of the Lord appeared to him in a dream and said, "Joseph son of David, do not be afraid to take Mary home as your wife, because what is conceived in her is from the Holy Spirit. She will give birth to a son, and you are to give him the name Jesus, because he will save his people from their sins."

MATTHEW 1:18–21

Israel in Jesus' Day

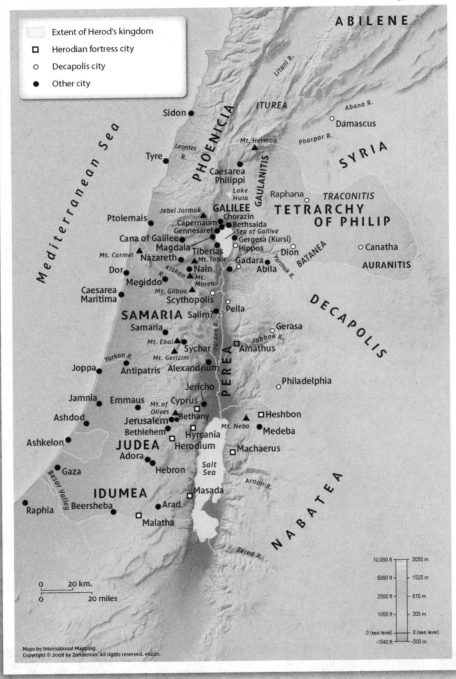

Legend:
- Extent of Herod's kingdom
- □ Herodian fortress city
- ○ Decapolis city
- ● Other city

ABILENE

Mediterranean Sea

PHOENICIA · ITUREA · Abana R. · Damascus

Sidon

Tyre · Leontes R. · Mt. Hermon · SYRIA · Pharpar R.

Caesarea Philippi · Lake Hula · GAULANITIS

Raphana · TRACONITIS

Jebel Jarmak · GALILEE · Chorazin · TETRARCHY OF PHILIP

Ptolemais · Capernaum · Bethsaida

Cana of Galilee · Gennesaret · Sea of Galilee · Gergesa (Kursi)

Magdala · Tiberias · Hippos · Dion · BATANEA · Canatha

Mt. Carmel · Nazareth · Mt. Tabor · Gadara · Abila · AURANITIS

Dor · Kishon R. · Nain · Mt. Moreh · Yarmuk R.

Megiddo · Mt. Gilboa

Caesarea Maritima · Scythopolis · DECAPOLIS

SAMARIA · Salim? · Pella

Samaria · Gerasa

Mt. Ebal · Sychar · Jabbok R. · Amathus

Yarkon R. · Mt. Gerizim · Jordan R.

Joppa · Antipatris · Alexandrium · Philadelphia

Jamnia · Emmaus · Cyprus · Jericho · PEREA

Ashdod · Mt. of Olives · Bethany · Heshbon

Jerusalem · Mt. Nebo · Medeba

Bethlehem · Hyrcania

Ashkelon · Herodium · Machaerus

JUDEA · Adora

Gaza · Hebron · Salt Sea · Arnon R. · NABATEA

IDUMEA · Masada

Raphia · Beersheba · Arad · Zered R.

Malatha

20 km.

20 miles

10,000 ft — 3050 m
5000 ft — 1525 m
2000 ft — 610 m
1000 ft — 305 m
0 (sea level) — 0 (sea level)
-1640 ft — -500 m

Maps by International Mapping.
Copyright © 2008 by Zondervan. All rights reserved. v0220.

Welcome | Read On Your Own

In the last session, you looked at the story of Joshua and saw how his zeal for the Lord, for God's Word, and for serving Moses set him apart from the other leaders in Israel. Joshua continued to demonstrate this zeal when God instructed him to cross the Jordan River and start to take back the Promised Land from the Canaanites. Eventually, the Israelites conquered *most* of the land, though not all of it. After Joshua's death, this cohabitation led the people to adopt the religious practices of these nations—with disastrous results.

Israel became a kingdom centuries later when God raised up Saul to serve as its first monarch. But it was only under the rule of his successor, David, that Israel became a powerful nation in the region. This "golden age" lasted only until the death of David's successor, his son Solomon, after which the country split into two kingdoms—Israel in the north and Judah in the south. Yet the problem of idolatry persisted, and ultimately God allowed the kingdoms to be conquered and the people taken away to foreign lands in exile.

However, as you saw in the first session, the exiles were able to return to Israel during the reign of Cyrus the Great of Persia. The Old Testament ends with the Jewish people resettling in the land. What follows are 400 years of "silence" in the Bible, during which time the world witnessed the fall of the Persian Empire at the hands of Alexander the Great, and the eventual rise of the mighty Roman Empire, which controlled most of the known world at the time the events of the New Testament begin to unfold.

It is at this point in Israel's history that God announces something extraordinary is about to happen. In this session, you will explore what that event was and how Mary, the young woman in the story, responded to that news from God. You will look at the challenges she faced and the sacrifices she made to be obedient to God. You will also examine the character traits that Mary possessed that enabled her to fulfill God's calling on her life . . . and how you can model those same traits in your life as you seek to follow after God.

Connect | 15 minutes

Welcome to session 6 of *The God of the How and When*. To get things started for this week's final group time, discuss one of the following questions:

- What is a key insight or takeaway from last week's personal study that you would like to share with the group?

— or —

- What are some of the qualities of a humble person? Who is someone in your life who has demonstrated these qualities of humility?

Watch | 20 minutes

Now watch the video for this session. As you watch, use the following outline to record any thoughts or concepts that stand out to you.

I. What was Mary's situation at the time the angel appeared to her?

    A. A young woman of teenage years like Mary would have been betrothed.

        1. There were two parts to a Jewish wedding. The first was the betrothal, where the groom would prepare a place for his bride. She would prepare herself for the wedding.

        2. According to Jewish law, betrothal was as binding as marriage. The only way to get out of a betrothal was through a certificate of divorce.

        3. If the betrothed parties were not faithful to one another, it was considered adultery under Jewish law, with all the penalties, shame, and stigma associated with it.

    B. Mary was betrothed to Joseph—engaged to be married and preparing herself for her big wedding day—when she experienced a divine interruption.

        1. An angel appeared to Mary and said that she was going to bear a son. When Mary stated that she had never been with a man and asked how this could be, the angel said that she would conceive through the power of the Holy Spirit (see Luke 1:30–34).

2. This was a real concern for Mary, as the consequences could have been life-long and tragic.

3. Mary responded in humility (see Luke 1:38). She could have gotten puffed up, thinking, "God chose me out of all the millions of women, so I must be special."

C. Joseph could not have taken Mary back if he had divorced her.

1. Under Jewish law, once a man divorces his wife, he can never take her back again. If Joseph had divorced Mary and learned later that he had made a mistake—that what he thought about her wasn't true—he never could have married her again.

2. For Mary, this would mean she had given birth to an illegitimate son, which carried with it all sorts of stigma. Jesus could not have been the Messiah if he were illegitimate.

D. Joseph responded to God in humble obedience as well.

1. Joseph would have now looked suspicious, because the implications would have been that he had relations with his betrothed before the actual wedding.

2. Joseph knew the prophecy in Isaiah 7:14 that "the virgin will conceive and give birth to a son, and will call him Immanuel." Part of the significance of the supernatural conception is that it points to the supernatural nature of the Messiah.

II. What else is significant about the divine names of the Messiah given in the Old Testament?

    A. The Isaiah 7:14 passage is tied to Isaiah 9:6–7, which gives divine names of the Messiah.

        1. The first part of the passage states, "He will be called Wonderful Counselor, Mighty God, Everlasting Father, Prince of Peace."

        2. The second part of the passage states, "Of the increase of His government . . . there will be no end" (NKJV). In the Hebrew, the phrase "of the increase of" is *lemarbeh*. It includes the Hebrew letter *mem* (which is the English letter "M" in Hebrew).

    B. The significance of the Hebrew letter *mem*.

        1. There are two forms of the letter *mem* in Hebrew.

            a. There is a closed letter *mem* that occurs at the end of a Hebrew word.

            b. There is an open letter *mem* that can occur anywhere else in a Hebrew word.

        2. In the phrase "of the increase of" in Isaiah 9:7, a closed *mem* appears in the word *le-marbeh* where an open *mem* would typically appear.

            a. A closed *mem* can symbolize a closed womb. The closed *mem* in "of the increase of" points to the fact that the virgin birth would be through a woman who has a closed womb, meaning it wasn't going to be a natural conception and birth.

            b. The rabbis say the open *mem* refers to the first redeemer, Moses, and the closed *mem* refers to the second redeemer, the Messiah. This is the closed *mem* in "of the increase of," ultimately pointing to the fact that Jesus was going to be the Messiah.

Divorce in the First Century

"This is how the birth of Jesus the Messiah came about: His mother Mary was pledged to be married to Joseph, but before they came together, she was found to be pregnant through the Holy Spirit. Because Joseph her husband was faithful to the law, and yet did not want to expose her to public disgrace, he had in mind to divorce her quietly" (Matthew 1:18–19).

The Law of Moses stipulated that a man could divorce his wife if he found "something indecent about her" and wrote out "a certificate of divorce" (Deuteronomy 24:1). However, once he issued that certificate of divorce, he could not take her back again if she had remarried. This was true regardless of whether her second husband divorced her or died (see verses 2–4). The law was intended to deter divorce, as it required the man to write a certificate—a public document—that granted the woman to remarry without sanction.

Women were not allowed to divorce their husbands for any reason. It is likely that many opted to escape such unpleasant situations by fleeing from their husband's home. There is at least one instance in the Bible of a woman leaving her husband and returning to the home of her parents (see Judges 19:1–4). But legally, the woman was bound to her husband as long as they both lived or until the man issued a public certificate of divorce.

We know from the story of Jesus' birth that at some point Mary revealed her pregnancy to Joseph. At that time, Joseph could have chosen to make her revelation of the pregnancy a public scandal. He could have brought her before the elders of the city, which would have led to her being publicly disgraced, or even forced her to go to the Temple in Jerusalem.

According to the the Law of Moses, a husband who suspected his wife of adultery could force her to undergo a a ceremony called the *sotah*. This was a "trial by ordeal" typical in many ancient Near Eastern cultures. The priests would take the name of God, write it on a piece of paper, dissolve it in water, and force her to drink it. If the water did not affect her, it proved she was faithful and the allegations were invalid. If she became ill, it proved she was guilty.

It is possible that Joseph could have subjected Mary to any of these elaborate and traumatic procedures. But Joseph had great humility and also great kindness. He was faithful to the Law of Moses but did not want Mary to endure public disgrate. So, he choose to divorce her "quietly." And when the angel of the Lord told him that the child had been conceived by the Holy Spirit, he humbly and willingly agreed to accept that child as his own.[39]

III. What do we learn from this story about Mary's character?

    A. Mary was kind and compassionate.

        1. Mary's name in Hebrew is Miriam. The name Miriam begins and ends with the letter *mem*.

        2. The letter *mem* is associated with water, with kindness, and with Miriam, Moses' sister. She was the embodiment of kindness in the Old Testament and is connected to water.

            a. Miriam was with Moses when their mother put him in a basket on the Nile. She watched over him as he went down into the water (see Exodus 2:3–4).

            b. Miriam picked up a timbrel after the Red Sea parted and began singing the "Shirat Hayam," the song of the sea, again associated with water (see Exodus 15:1–18).

            c. Mary's name means "bitter waters." So her name itself is associated with water.

        3. Mary is associated with water and kindness, as seen in the story of the wedding at Cana.

            a. Mary comes to Jesus at the wedding and asks him to do something about the wine that had run out (see John 2:1–3).

            b. Mary is concerned about the bride and the groom. If they were to run out of wine at the wedding, it would result in tremendous shame, because hospitality was a huge thing in Jewish and Middle Eastern culture.

    c. Mary's kindness is seen by her being concerned in connection with the water.

B. Mary also demonstrated *chutzpah*—holy audacity or boldness.

    1. We think of humility and *chutzpah* as opposites, but they are two sides of the same coin.

    2. We see this combination of humility and *chutzpah* in this story. When Mary comes to Jesus and says that he has to do something about the situation, he responds, "Woman, what does your concern have to do with me?" (John 2:4). But Mary does not take no for an answer.

    3. There is nothing humbler than being bold and fulfilling what God has asked us to do or what we know to be right. We see this humility and boldness coming together in Mary.

IV. What are some of the other challenges that Mary had to face as Jesus grew up?

    A. Mary had to demonstrate sacrificial obedience.

        1. There was a cost for being faithful to God. She would have endured scorn and shame for being a woman who became pregnant before the wedding.

        2. But her greatest challenge was that she knew her son, Jesus, was the Messiah—and yet it was thirty years before he revealed himself.

Miriam and Mary

The name Mary in Hebrew is Miriam. In the Old Testament, Miriam was the sister of Moses and Aaron and is connected with *water* and with *kindness*—two traits also associated with Mary, the mother of Jesus, in the New Testament. These traits are connected with Miriam because of the events that occur when we are first introduced to her in the Bible.

The king of Egypt was wary of the rising Israelite population and feared they would join with the nation's enemies if a war broke out. So he commanded the Hebrew midwives to kill any Hebrew baby boy. When these godly women refused to go along with the plan, the king decreed that all Hebrew baby boys be thrown into the Nile. When Moses was born, his mother hid him for three months and then placed him in a papyrus basket. She placed him where he would be found in the waters of the Nile. Miriam stood at a distance and watched.

When the king's own daughter discovered the child, Miriam demonstrated her kindness by intervening and offering to get one of the Hebrew women to nurse the baby. This quick thinking on her part meant that Moses was raised by his mother in infancy. After he had grown older, the king's daughter took him and raised him as her own. She is the one who gave him the name Moses, which means, "I drew him out of the water" (see Exodus 1:8–2:10).

Miriam makes several other appearances in the Bible. Years later, after God parted the waters of the Red Sea so the Israelites could escape the Egyptians, she encouraged the other Israelite women to join her in giving praise to God for his deliverance (see 15:20–21). Miriam is here regarded as a prophet, a title that reveals her role in shepherding the people. But some time later, we read that Miriam grew jealous that God had Moses put in charge of leading the Israelites and spoke out against him. This led to her being struck with leprosy. Moses pleaded with God on her behalf, and she was healed (see Numbers 12:5–16).[40]

The rabbis say that Israel was redeemed from Egypt only through the merit of righteous women. In the Exodus story, it was the Hebrew midwives who refused to kill the baby boys who were the heroes. It was the daughter of Pharoah, who took compassion on Moses, who was the hero. It was Moses' mother, who came up with a plan to save her baby's life, who was the hero. And it was Miriam, the sister who intervened for her brother, who was the hero of the story.

3. Mary faced challenges when Jesus was on the cross and in the grave. Just imagine what that would have been like. "God, you made this promise to me . . . and is this really how it ends?"

4. Mary was long-suffering in her willingness to wait to see God's promises and plans fulfilled.

B. Just like Miriam in the Old Testament was there for Moses, so Mary and the women were there for Jesus, playing a central role in the story of redemption.

1. One of the first people at the tomb after the resurrection was Mary Magdalene (see John 20:1–18). She was one of the first to announce the gospel.

2. Women were the first evangelists. It is important to understand the significance of women in God's role of redemption and how Jesus elevated women.

C. How do we apply Mary's story to our lives today?

1. Mary responded to God in humility and obedience. We need to be willing to do the same.

2. Mary was willing to pay the price and give birth to the Son of God. When we are also willing to pay the price to follow God, he can birth something significant and beautiful through us.

Discuss | 35 minutes

Take some time to discuss what you just watched by answering the following questions. There are some suggested questions below to help you begin your discussion, but feel free to pick any of the additional questions as well as time allows.

Suggested Questions

1. Mary would have likely been a teenager when she was betrothed to Joseph. According to Jewish law, betrothal was as binding as marriage, and if one of the parties was not faithful to the other, it was considered *adultery*. In spite of this, how did Mary respond when the angel announced that she would conceive through the power of the Holy Spirit and give birth to a son?

2. Joseph was going to divorce Mary quietly when he learned that she was pregnant. However, he went through with the marriage after the angel of the Lord visited him in a dream and said the child was conceived by the Holy Spirit. What risks was Joseph taking in doing this? What public humiliation would he have faced for this decision?

3. Mary demonstrated great kindness in the story of the wedding at Cana. She understood that if the bride and groom were to run out of wine at the festivities, it would result in tremendous shame for the couple and their families. How did she alert Jesus about the problem? How did she demonstrate her faith that he would act?

4. Mary's obedience to God required sacrifice. She endured scorn for being a woman who became pregnant before her wedding. She had to wait thirty years before her son

revealed himself as the Messiah. What was the greatest sacrifice that she had to make? What does it say about Mary's character that she was willing to make these sacrifices?

Additional Questions

5. When the angel told Mary that she would give birth to the Son of God, she could have gotten puffed up and responded to the news with pride. But how instead did Mary react? What does her response teach us about how we should respond to God?

6. Read Isaiah 9:7. In the Hebrew, the phrase "of the increase of" contains a closed Hebrew letter *mem* where an open *mem* would typically appear. What could this closed *mem* signify? How is this significant in the angel's announcement to Mary?

7. Mary not only demonstrated kindness in the story of the wedding at Cana but also *chutzpah*—which can be defined as holy audacity or boldness. In what way was Mary bold in her request to Jesus? How do you think this impacted Jesus' decision to act?

8. Mary responded to God in humility and obedience. She was willing to pay the price and give birth to the Son of God. What does her story say about the things that God can "birth" in us when we likewise respond to his call with humility and obedience?

Respond | 10 minutes

Review the outline for the video teaching and any notes you took. In the space below, write down your most significant takeaway from this session.

Pray | 10 minutes

End your time by praying together as a group, asking the Lord to help you better respond to him in humility. Ask if anyone has any prayer requests to share. Write those requests down in the space below so you and your group members can pray about them in the week ahead.

Name   Request

Personal Study

As you have seen in this study, God does not always reveal the *how* and *when* of his plans when he asks his followers to step out in faith. Mary certainly didn't receive all the details when the angel announced that she would give birth to the Messiah. She must have wondered where this divine disruption in her life would lead. Yet she chose to respond to God's call with obedience and humility. When you do the same, you never know what amazing things that God will birth in you. As you explore these themes in the life of Mary this week, be sure to write down your responses to the questions in the spaces provided, as you will be given a few minutes to share your insights at the start of the next session if you are doing this study with others. If you are reading *The God of the Way* alongside this study, first review chapter 5 in the book.

- Day 1 -

Called to Scandal?

Unlike Abraham, Sarah, Moses, and Joshua, when Mary was called by God, she was not in her later years. She was a teenager. And she was betrothed to a man named Joseph. This would have been typical of a woman of her age during the time. Unlike engagements today, betrothal was a binding agreement.[41] Her role during the betrothal period was to remain pure and then prove that purity when the time for marriage arrived.[42]

If you know anything about Mary's story, what God called her to do would have seriously put the reputation of her purity in jeopardy. She would be at serious risk of Joseph ending the engagement—something the Bible says that he was planning on doing—and the end of her social acceptance. If anyone had the right to ask God *how,* it was Mary.

How will I give birth to the Son of God when I am a virgin? How will I prove to Joseph I've remained pure when I am clearly pregnant? How will I prove this to my family and my community? How is anyone going to believe that this child is conceived by the Holy Spirit?

While Abraham, Sarah, Moses, and Joshua were called to greatness—founding, freeing, and leading the nation of Israel—it seemed that Mary was called to knowingly enter what would have been considered a major scandal in her time . . . with her at the center of it. How could God ask this of her? Only he could answer that question.

Read | Luke 1:26–38

Reflect

1. Joseph was a descendant of David, which is important, as the Messiah had been prophesied to come through David's line. What did Gabriel promise Mary?

2. The angel told Mary that her child would be called "Son of the Most High" (verse 32) and that the Lord would give him the throne of his ancestor David. What was Mary's response to this promise? How did she demonstrate her humility in this response?

3. Have you ever experienced or witnessed a "scandal" or scenario of which your family disapproved? If you have experienced this firsthand, what was that experience like for you? If you were a witness, what did you think about the people involved?

4. In hindsight, where can you see God at work in this situation? What does the story of Mary reveal about the way that the God of the How and When works in this world?

Pray | You may not feel that you are always as obedient to your calling as Mary was to hers. It won't always be easy to accept the scenarios in which you find yourself. But regardless of wherever you are today, take a few minutes to speak honestly about it with your heavenly Father.

Jesus or Immanuel? *"The virgin will conceive and give birth to a son, and will call him Immanuel"* (Isaiah 7:14). This prophecy reveals the Messiah would be called *Immanuel*. But when the Savior is born, he is named *Jesus*. Why the difference? The name *Immanuel* means "God with us," so the prophecy simply means that God would be dwelling with his people in the person of the Messiah. Isaiah gives other names that Jesus will be called that also reflect attributes of his nature: "He will be called Wonderful Counselor, Mighty God, Everlasting Father, Prince of Peace" (Isaiah 9:6).[43]

- Day 2 -

Strength from a Friend

After the angel Gabriel visited Mary, she went to visit her relative Elizabeth, who had miraculously become pregnant at an old age after many years of being childless. When Elizabeth saw Mary, her "baby leaped in her womb" (Luke 1:42), and she said, "Blessed are you among women, and blessed is the child you will bear! But why am I so favored, that the mother of my Lord should come to me?" (verses 42–43).

Put yourself in Mary's shoes for a moment. You're a teenager who has just been told she will become pregnant with the Son of God while still a virgin. You want to obey God, but you're afraid. You're still asking, *"How can this be?"* So you've gone to visit a trusted relative. She is older and wiser than you. Her faith is stronger because it's endured years of hardship. When she sees you, she already knows what's happened to you. She doesn't doubt you or your story. She simply believes and, more than that, she affirms you. She calls you blessed!

Mary responded to Elizabeth with a song that you will read in today's study. Her words give us a glimpse into how the visit must have made her feel. She stayed on with Elizabeth for three months—likely long enough for Elizabeth to give birth to her son, John the Baptist.[44] Perhaps Mary needed this time to rest and let the reality of what the angel had told her sink in. And perhaps watching Elizabeth's miracle come true helped her believe in her own.

Read | Luke 1:46–55

Reflect

1. The song of Mary is also known as the *Magnificat*, which is Latin for "my soul glorifies the Lord" (verse 46). It is widely regarded as one of the eight most ancient Christian hymns. How would you describe Mary's tone in this song?

2. Mary states, "From now on all generations will call me blessed, for the Mighty One has done great things for me" (verses 48–49). How does Mary go on to describe God?

3. Elizabeth gave Mary the affirmation and support that she needed at a difficult time. Who is an Elizabeth in your life—someone who has gone before you and given you courage to keep going? How has this person encouraged your faith journey?

4. Read 1 Thessalonians 5:16–18. Mary knew that she would endure a great deal of social scorn for the pregnancy, yet she was still able to praise God. What does this tell us about her faith? What does it look like in your life to give thanks in *all* circumstances?

Pray | Spend a few moments in prayer. If you need an Elizabeth in your life, ask God to send one to you. If you have one, express gratitude for this person's encouragement and guidance.

— Day 3 —

In Her Heart

The angel told Mary she would give birth to the Son of the Most High, but Jesus' divinity was not revealed right away. It would be thirty-three years before he began his public ministry. In the meantime, Mary had to *wait*.

Mary didn't know how or when Jesus would reveal himself, but she saw signs along the way. Shepherds came to Jesus' manger at his birth, telling of an angel who said the Messiah had been born (see Luke 2:11–12). When Jesus was twelve years old, his parents lost him in the city of Jerusalem during the Festival of the Passover. When they found him, he was teaching in the temple—much to the amazement of the teachers (see Luke 2:41–48).

The Bible tells us that after each of these events, Mary pondered these things in her heart (see Luke 2:19, 51). It doesn't say that she witnessed these things and shouted them from the rooftop. It doesn't say she spread the word among her friends and neighbors. It simply says that she treasured these things and held them close to her heart.

Has anything ever caused you to ponder it in your heart? A touching moment, a glimpse of the future, a dream? Something you knew was important, but you weren't sure why, so you quietly stored it away? Sometimes God blesses us with moments we can't wait to share. But sometimes he blesses us with moments that are just for us . . . at least for now.

Read | Luke 2:8–19, 41–52

Reflect

1. Shepherds held a lowly place in Jewish society. They were generally considered untrustworthy and their work made them ceremonially unclean. What do you think is the significance of the angel announcing the birth of the Messiah to this group?

2. What do these stories reveal about Jesus? Which details from these two stories do you imagine Mary most treasured and pondered in her heart?

3. Sometimes God reveals moments like these to us . . . times in our lives when we get glimpses of his plans and purposes on this earth. What are some moments like these in your life that you have treasured in your heart? Why where they meaningful to you?

4. There is no record in the Gospels that Mary revealed these things to others. How do you decide when to keep a moment like this to yourself and when to tell others about it?

Pray | Spend a few moments in prayer. Ponder the moments, promises, and blessings that God has given to you this week.

The Visit of the Magi.
Nativity scenes typically picture Jesus lying in a manger surrounded by Mary and Joseph, shepherds, and the three wise men. But the "wise men," or, more accurately, the Magi (members of a priestly caste in ancient Persia), were not present at the time of Jesus' birth. An early church tradition placed their arrival at thirteen days after his birth, but modern historians believe it was one to two years later. Furthermore, we also don't know how many Magi there were. The number three is typically given because of the three gifts they brought (see Matthew 2:9–12).

-Day 4-

Chutzpah

We tend to imagine Mary as meek, humble, quiet, and lowly. While Mary certainly exuded humility, she also exhibited strength and audacity. This is particularly true in the story you will read today that describes Jesus' first miracle—for which, in a way, Mary was responsible.

Mary had what we might call *chutzpah*, which can be defined as "holy boldness and audacity."[45] When the wedding that she, Jesus, and the disciples were attending in Cana ran out of wine, she knew exactly who could fix the problem: her son. What's more she didn't hesitate for a moment to ask him for his help—not because she enjoyed being bossy, but because she didn't doubt Jesus' ability and power. She knew who he was and trusted him.

When we likewise know who Jesus is and trust him, we will be much bolder in our prayers and in our actions. We ask God for what we need not because we are being high and mighty and think we deserve it, but simply because we know that God can provide it for us. We step into our callings, and out of our comfort zones, not because we think we are so capable and talented and gifted and whatever else, but because we know that in Christ we are enough, and he isn't going to begin a work in us that he won't finish.

This is the essence of *chutzpah*—boldly believing in Jesus. Mary had it because she knew Jesus. We have it because we have known him too.

Read | John 2:1–11

Reflect

1. We don't know the relationship between Mary and the bride and groom getting married in Cana, but it was close enough that she felt the need to get involved

when the festivities ran out of wine. How did Mary indicate to Jesus that there was a problem? How did she respond when Jesus said that his time had not yet come?

2. When the master of the banquet tasted the wine, he said the bride and groom had "saved the best till now" (verse 10)—which reveals the abundant way that God provides for his children. What impact did this miracle have (see verse 11)?

3. Think of a time you exhibited *chutzpah*—holy boldness. What inspired you to be bold?

4. Where might you be lacking in *chutzpah* in your life? What might be some of the reasons as to why you are stepping back instead of stepping up in that area?

Pray | Be bold in your prayer time today. Tap into Mary's trust and belief in Jesus and ask him for what you *really* need. Then thank God for his abundant provision in your life.

Day 5

At the Cross

Mary witnessed Jesus in glory and witnessed him in tragedy. The Bible tells us that she was "near the cross" as he hung there and as he died. It doesn't tell us what she was thinking or how she was feeling. But any parent who has lost a child can connect those dots. Mary believed in her son's divinity, but that would not make the pain of losing him any less.

Perhaps she had seen this day coming. She knew what happened to those who went against the status quo or were perceived as rabble-rousers. Rome had little tolerance for renegades who might stir up the people and spark a revolution. Rebels were handled swiftly . . . often by crucifixion. Still, what could have prepared her for what she saw on that day?

After all, what prepared you for tragedy, heartbreak, or loss that you experienced? Who, or what, have you watched die, feeling helpless and devastated? A child, a loved one, a dream? Mary felt this pain. Even if the hope of resurrection had been buried in her heart, the pain she felt would not be diminished by future joy. It was *real*, and she was present with it. She didn't run from the cross. She stood near it. She watched the life of her beloved son pass.

Christians often offer platitudes in the face of death. *At least he's in heaven. At least you'll see him again someday. Maybe this is for the best.* But these platitudes offer little when you are in the throes of grief—and that's okay. You don't have to bypass your pain. Hope and pain can coexist, just as they did for Mary as she stood at the foot of Jesus' cross.

Read | John 19:16–27

Reflect

1. The Gospels state that Jesus was crucified at the order of Pontius Pilate, the Roman governor of Judea, and that he hung between two criminals. But who does John state in this passage was standing at the foot of Jesus' cross?

2. Scholars believe the reference to "the disciple whom [Jesus] loved" (verse 26) was John, which means this was a firsthand account. What were Jesus' instructions to John regarding his mother? What does this tell you about Mary and Jesus' relationship?

3. Crucifixion was an agonizing death that typically lasted for hours. In Jesus' case, the Gospels reveal that he hung on the cross for *six hours* . . . and Mary was with him. When have you sat at the foot of a cross and experienced the pain as Mary did? What or whom were you grieving?

4. What is a grief or pain that you've tried to bypass or overlook in your life? What would it look like to sit with that pain instead of running from it?

Pray | Spend a few minutes reflecting on this week's personal study time. Did God convict you of anything this week? Did you change in any way or learn something new? Talk to God about what you discovered in his Word this week and what he might be showing you today.

Leader's Guide

Thank you for your willingness to lead your group through this study! What you have chosen to do is valuable and will make a great difference in the lives of others. *The God of the How and When* is a six-session Bible study built around video content and small-group interaction. As the group leader, imagine yourself as the host of a party. Your job is to take care of your guests by managing the details so that when your guests arrive, they can focus on one another and on the topic for that session.

Your role as the group leader is not to answer all the questions or reteach the content—the video, book, and study guide will do most of that work. Your job is to guide the experience and cultivate your small group into a connected and engaged community. This will make it a place for members to process, question, and reflect—not necessarily receive more instruction.

There are several elements in this leader's guide that will help you as you structure your study and reflection time, so be sure to follow along and take advantage of each one.

Before You Begin

Before your first meeting, make sure the group members have a copy of this study guide. Alternately, you can hand out the study guides at your first meeting and give the members some time to look over the material and ask any preliminary questions. Also make sure they are aware that they have access to the streaming videos at any time by following the instructions printed on the inside front cover. During your first meeting, ask the members to provide their name, phone number, and email address so you can keep in touch with them.

Generally, the ideal size for a group is eight to ten people, which will ensure that everyone has enough time to participate in discussions. If you have more people, you might want to break up the main group into smaller subgroups. Encourage those who show up at the first meeting to commit to attending for the duration of the study, as this will help the group members get to know one another, create stability for the group, and help you know how to best prepare to lead them through the material.

Each of the sessions begins with an opening reflection in the "Welcome" section. The questions that follow in the "Connect" section serve as an icebreaker to get the group members thinking about the topic. Some people may want to tell a long story in response to one of these questions, but the goal is to keep the answers brief. Ideally, you want everyone in the group to get a chance to answer, so try to keep the responses to a minute or less. If you have talkative group members, say up front that everyone needs to limit their answer to one minute.

Give the group members a chance to answer, but also tell them to feel free to pass if they wish. With the rest of the study, it's generally not a good idea to have everyone answer every question—a free-flowing discussion is more desirable. But with the opening icebreaker questions, you can go around the circle. Encourage shy people to share, but don't force them.

At your first meeting, let the group members know each session contains a personal study section they can use to continue to engage with the content until the next meeting. While this is optional, it will help them cement the concepts presented during the group study time and help them better understand the character, nature, and attributes of the God of the How and When. Let them know that if they choose to do so, they can watch the video for the next session by accessing the streaming code found on the inside front cover of their studies. Invite them to bring any questions and insights to your next meeting, especially if they had a breakthrough moment or didn't understand something.

Preparation for Each Session

As the leader, there are a few things you should do to prepare for each meeting:

- **Read through the session.** This will help you become more familiar with the content and know how to structure the discussion times.

- **Decide how the videos will be used.** Determine whether you want the members to watch the videos ahead of time (again, via the streaming access code found on the inside front cover) or together as a group.

- **Decide which questions you want to discuss.** Based on the length of your group discussions, you may not be able to get through all the questions. So look over the recommendations for the suggested and additional questions in each session and choose which ones you definitely want to cover.

- **Be familiar with the questions you want to discuss.** When the group meets, you'll be watching the clock, so make sure you are familiar with the questions that you have selected. In this way, you will ensure that you have the material more deeply in your mind than your group members.

- **Pray for your group.** Pray for your group members and ask God to lead them as they study his Word.

In many cases, there will be no one "right" answer to the question. Answers will vary, especially when the group members are being asked to share their personal experiences.

Structuring the Discussion Time

You will need to determine with your group how long you want to meet so you can plan your time accordingly. Suggested times for each section have been provided in this study guide, and if you adhere to these times, your group will meet for ninety minutes, as noted below. If you want to meet for two hours, follow the times given in the right-hand column:

Section	90 Minutes	120 Minutes
CONNECT (discuss one or more of the opening questions for the session)	15 minutes	20 minutes
WATCH (watch the teaching material together and take notes)	20 minutes	20 minutes
DISCUSS (discuss the study questions you selected ahead of time)	35 minutes	50 minutes
RESPOND (write down key takeaways)	10 minutes	15 minutes
PRAY (pray together and dismiss)	10 minutes	15 minutes

As the group leader, it is up to you to keep track of the time and keep things on schedule. You might want to set a timer for each segment so both you and the group members know when your time is up. Don't be concerned if the group members are quiet or slow to share. People are often quiet when they are pulling together their ideas, and this might be a new experience for them. Just ask a question and let it hang in the air until someone shares. You can then say, "Thank you. What about others? What came to you when you watched that portion of the teaching?"

Group Dynamics

Leading a group through *The God of the How and When* will prove to be highly rewarding both to you and your group members. But you still may encounter challenges along the way! Discussions can get off track. Group members may not be sensitive to the needs and ideas of others. Some might worry they will be expected to talk about matters that make them feel awkward. Others may express comments that result in disagreements. To help ease this strain on you and the group, consider the following ground rules:

- When someone raises a question or comment that is off the main topic, suggest that you deal with it another time, or, if you feel led to go in that direction, let the group know you will be spending some time discussing it.

- If someone asks a question that you don't know how to answer, admit it and move on. At your discretion, feel free to invite group members to comment on questions that call for personal experience.

- If you find one or two people are dominating the discussion time, direct a few questions to others in the group. Outside the main group time, ask the more dominating members to help you draw out the quieter ones. Work to make them a part of the solution instead of part of the problem.

- When a disagreement occurs, encourage the group members to process the matter in love. Encourage those on opposite sides to restate what they heard the other side say about the matter, and then invite each side to evaluate if that perception is accurate. Lead the group in examining other Scriptures related to the topic and look for common ground.

When any of these issues arise, encourage your group members to follow these words from Scripture: "Love one another" (John 13:34); "If it is possible, as far as it depends on you, live at peace with everyone" (Romans 12:18); and, "Be quick to listen, slow to speak and slow to become angry" (James 1:19). This will make your group time more rewarding and beneficial for everyone who attends.

Thank you again for taking the time to lead your group. You are making a difference in your group members' lives and having an impact on their journey toward a better understanding of the God of the How and When.

Endnotes

1. J. I. Packer, Merrill C. Tenney, and William White Jr., *The Land of the Bible* (Nashville, TN: Thomas Nelson, 1985), 26.
2. Whitney Woollard, "The Land: A Thermometer of Covenantal Faithfulness," Bible Project, https://bibleproject.com/blog/land-thermometer-covenantal-faithfulness/.
3. Woollard, "The Land: A Thermometer of Covenantal Faithfulness," Bible Project, https://bibleproject.com/blog/land-thermometer-covenantal-faithfulness/.
4. Rabbi Jason Sobel, *Mysteries of the Messiah: Unveiling Divine Connections from Genesis to Today* (Nashville, TN: W Publishing, 2021), 39.
5. James B. Pritchard, ed., *Ancient Near Eastern Texts Relating to the Old Testament*, 3rd ed. (Princeton, NJ: Princeton, 1969), 532.
6. Pritchard, ed., *Ancient Near Eastern Texts Relating to the Old Testament*, 222–223.
7. Jenny Phillips, "Jesus and Wilderness," American Bible Society, https://bibleresources.americanbible.org/resource/jesus-and-wilderness.
8. Phillips, "Jesus and Wilderness," American Bible Society, https://bibleresources.americanbible.org/resource/jesus-and-wilderness.
9. Woollard, "The Land: A Thermometer of Covenantal Faithfulness," Bible Project, https://bibleproject.com/blog/land-thermometer-covenantal-faithfulness/.
10. Woollard, "The Land: A Thermometer of Covenantal Faithfulness," Bible Project, https://bibleproject.com/blog/land-thermometer-covenantal-faithfulness/.
11. Malachi Martin, "Footsteps of Abraham," *The New York Times,* https://www.nytimes.com/1983/03/13/travel/footsteps-of-abraham-by-malachi-martin.html.
12. Ashley Hooker, "What Is the Feast of the Trumpets?", Bible Study Tools, https://www.biblestudytools.com/bible-study/topical-studies/what-is-the-feast-of-trumpets.html.
13. John H. Walton, Victor H. Matthews, and Mark W. Chavalas, *The IVP Bible Background Commentary: Old Testament* (Downers Grove, IL: IVP Academic), 43.
14. John H. Sailhamer, *The Expositor's Bible Commentary: Genesis* (Grand Rapids, MI: Zondervan Academic, 2008), 169.
15. Kathie Lee Gifford, and Rabbi Jason Sobel, *The God of the Way* (Nashville, TN: W Publishing, 2022), 20.
16. Walton, et al, *The IVP Bible Background Commentary: Old Testament* (Downers Grove, IL: IVP Academic), 53.
17. "What Is the Significance of Mount Moriah in the Bible?", Got Questions, https://www.gotquestions.org/mount-Moriah.html.
18. B. Megillah 15a (New York, Columbia University, Butler Library, x 893-t), 141.
19. Walton, et al, *The IVP Bible Background Commentary: Old Testament* (Downers Grove, IL: IVP Academic), 43.
20. Cynthia R. Chapman, "Barrenness," Bible Odyssey, https://www.bibleodyssey.org/en/people/related-articles/barrenness.
21. J. I. Packer, Merrill C. Tenney, and William White Jr., *Daily Life in Bible Times* (Nashville, TN: Thomas Nelson, 1982), 63-64.
22. Sailhamer, *The Expositor's Bible Commentary: Genesis* (Grand Rapids, MI: Zondervan Academic, 2008), 169.
23. Sailhamer, *The Expositor's Bible Commentary: Genesis* (Grand Rapids, MI: Zondervan Academic, 2008), 205.
24. Walton, et al, *The IVP Bible Background Commentary: Old Testament* (Downers Grove, IL: IVP Academic), 43.
25. "A Closer Look at the Nerves in Your Feet," PMC Foot and Ankle Clinic, https://www.pmcfootandankleclinic.com/blog/a-closer-look-at-the-nerves-in-your-feet.
26. Packer, et al, *Daily Life in Bible Times* (Nashville, TN: Thomas Nelson, 1982), 136–137.
27. "Why Was Moses Punished for Striking the Rock?", Verse By Verse Ministry, https://www.versebyverseministry.org/bible-answers/why-was-moses-punished-for-striking-the-rock.
28. Walton, et al, *The IVP Bible Background Commentary: Old Testament* (Downers Grove, IL: IVP Academic), 79.
29. James Strong, *Strong's Exhaustive Concordance of the Bible*, Hebrew # 6944, https://www.biblestudytools.com/lexicons/hebrew/nas/qodesh.html.
30. Andreas Köstenberger, *The Expositor's Bible Commentary: 2 Timothy* (Grand Rapids, MI: Zondervan Academic, 2006), 570.
31. Daniel Esparza, "Moses, Elijah, and Jesus: Why Are They All Together at the Transfiguration?", https://aleteia.org/2019/03/17/moses-elijah-and-jesus-why-are-they-all-together-at-the-transfiguration/.
32. "Can Sheep Live Without a Shepherd?" Farming Base, https://farmingbase.com/can-sheep-live-without-a-shepherd/#:~:text=Sheep%20cannot%20live%20without%20the,and%20greatly%20endanger%20their%20lives.

33. "What Was a Shepherd in the Bible?" Got Questions, https://www.gotquestions.org/shepherd-in-the-Bible.html.
34. "What Is Biblical Typology?" Got Questions, https://www.gotquestions.org/typology-Biblical.html.
35. Wayne Jackson, "A Study of Biblical Types," Christian Courier, https://www.christiancourier.com/articles/126-a-study-of-biblical-types.
36. Packer, et al, *Daily Life in Bible Times* (Nashville, TN: Thomas Nelson, 1982), 84–90.
37. Gifford and Sobel, *The God of the Way* (Nashville, TN: Thomas Nelson, 2022), 49.
38. "Joshua," Chabad.org, https://www.chabad.org/library/article_cdo/aid/129625/jewish/Joshua.htm.
39. Packer, et al, *Daily Life in Bible Times* (Nashville, TN: Thomas Nelson, 1982), 53–54.
40. "Miriam: The Woman Who Helped Save a Nation," The Basilica, https://www.nationalshrine.org/blog/miriam-the-woman-who-helped-save-a-nation/.
41. Omar C. Garcia, "Bible Teaching Notes, Matthew 1:18," https://bibleteachingnotes.blog/2018/09/15/matthew-1/.
42. Gifford and Sobel, *The God of the Way* (Nashville, TN: Thomas Nelson, 2022), 62.
43. "Why Wasn't Jesus Named Immanuel?" Got Questions, https://www.gotquestions.org/Immanuel-Jesus.html.
44. Walton, et al, *The IVP Bible Background Commentary: Old Testament* (Downers Grove, IL: IVP Academic), 191.
45. Gifford and Sobel, *The God of the Way* (Nashville, TN: Thomas Nelson, 2022), 66.

ALSO AVAILABLE

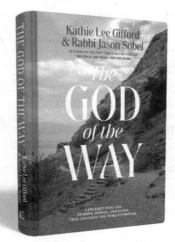

The God the Way
ISBN 9780785290438
On sale September 2022

The God of His Word
ISBN 9780310156673
On sale December 2022

The God of the How and When
ISBN 9780310156543
On sale November 2022

The God Who Sees
ISBN 9780310156802
On sale July 2023

The God of the Other Side
ISBN 9780310156932
On sale January 2024

Available wherever books are sold

 W PUBLISHING GROUP

 Harper*Christian* Resources